FROZEN FURY

The Murmansk Run of Convoy PQ-13

by

John L. Haynes

PublishAmerica
Baltimore

© 2010 by John L. Haynes.
All rights reserved. No part of this book may be reproduced, stored in a retrieval system or transmitted in any form or by any means without the prior written permission of the publishers, except by a reviewer who may quote brief passages in a review to be printed in a newspaper, magazine or journal.

First printing

PublishAmerica has allowed this work to remain exactly as the author intended, verbatim, without editorial input.

Hardcover 978-1-4512-0157-4
Softcover 978-1-4512-0156-7
PUBLISHED BY PUBLISHAMERICA, LLLP
www.publishamerica.com
Baltimore

Printed in the United States of America

*This story is dedicated to the memory of my mother,
who spent untold hours on her knees in prayer for me.
I believe God answered those prayers and kept me safe
during the perilous times of war and other dangers.
I thank God daily for His care and blessings.*

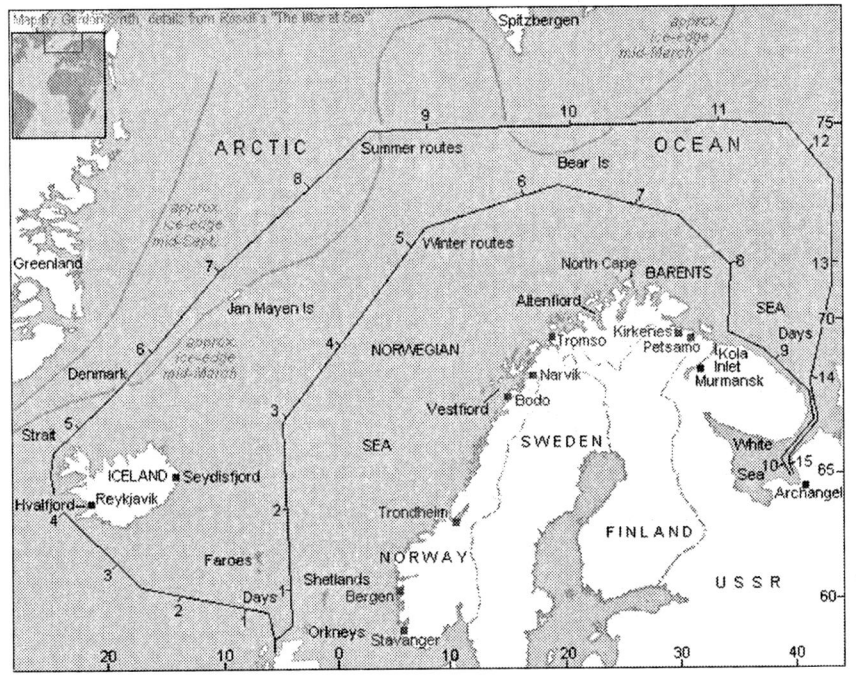

CONTENTS

PREFACE 9
INTRODUCTION 11
Chapter 1
THE EARLY YEARS 15
Chapter 2
WORLD WAR II BEGINS 19
Chapter 3
THE VOYAGE BEGINS 22
Chapter 4
CONVOY PQ-13 27
Chapter 5
JIG HOW 31
Chapter 6
MURMANSK 37
Chapter 7
ASHORE & MORE RAIDS 56
Chapter 8
CONVOY QP-11 LEAVES MURMANDSK 61
Chapter 9
HOMEWARD BOUND 65
Chapter 10
STATESIDE DUTY 70
Chapter 11
FLYING HIGH 74
Appendix I 81
Appendix II 86
Appendix III 88

ACKNOWLEDGMENTS

I deeply appreciate the patience, understanding, and support of my wife, Juanita, in this endeavor. This year we celebrate our 64th anniversary. Our daughter, Marie Miller, spent many hours with me in editing my typing and composition, as well as making many suggestions for improvements. All four of our children, Marie, John II, Renita, and Robert have been a source of enduring encouragement.

To my fellow British seafarer, Morris O. Mills, who sailed with us in the *New Westminster City* and wrote the wonderful book, *Convoy PQ13 Unlucky for Some* I owe a debt of gratitude. We shared a great many experiences even though we were on different ships. His writings stirred my memory of many events that I might otherwise have missed. The *New Westminster City* was bombed while offloading in the port of Murmansk, leaving it a total loss and costing many lives. Mills himself lost a foot and spent most of April 1942 in a Murmansk makeshift hospital. He sailed with us in the departure convoy QP-11 on the HMS *Edinburgh* as an evacuee. Tragically this ship was lost as well. He spent many more months in Russian hospitals before finally returning to England. Morris Mills, thank you for your service and your book.

A special thanks to Charles A. Lloyd, Chairman, U.S. Naval Armed Guard Veterans of World War II and publisher of *The Pointer*; Ron Carlson, Webmaster of Armed Guard website www.armed-guard; Captain Steve C. Myers, USN, for his *"Murmansk Run"* poem; my friend, Roy Brown, author of *Jig How*; and many other friends on the Armed Guard and Merchant Marine Message Board.

PREFACE

This story is a true account of my Naval service during World War II. Every effort has been made to be factual in the reporting of events, especially during the first six months from December 1941 through June 1942. It was during this period and beyond that Great Britton and the United States shipped millions of tons of vital war materials to the Soviet Union under a Lend Lease Agreement.

Merchant ships—some of which were "Rust Buckets" built in the early 1900s and others that were newly constructed "Liberty" ships—were all used in large convoys for delivery. The convoys were escorted by British and American Navy cruisers, destroyers, corvettes, trawlers and tugs to offer protection against German submarines (U-boats), surface raiders and aircraft. The U.S. Navy began arming the American merchant ships and assigning Naval Armed Guard gun crews to these ships to offer additional protection.

Convoy PQ-13 was one of the early convoys of 1942. The SS *Eldena*, the ship on which I served, was a 6900 ton, flush deck freighter, built in 1919, and was one of the "Rust Buckets" sailing. Her voyage began February 11th from Boston to Halifax to Scotland where Convoy PQ-13 was formed. Of the twenty ships in the convoy, ten were American, and of that ten only the SS *Dunboyne*, SS *Effingham*, SS *Mormacma* and SS *Eldena* had Naval Armed Guard gun crews aboard. The convoy departed Scotland March 10th via Iceland and arrived in Murmansk, Russia March 30th.

During this leg of the voyage the convoy endured horrendous winter storms and ice floes that choked and damaged the ships. It was attacked by German U-boats, surface raiders and air attacks resulting in the loss of several ships. In port in Murmansk eight to ten daily air raids were not uncommon: the town was pounded and more ships were destroyed. The return voyage was more of the same. Of the original twenty ships, twelve were lost; 5 American, 5 British, 1 Polish and 1 Russian.

Extensive research was made of British and American historical records. Internet sources as well as a number of history books, archive reports, and personal accounts were used for accuracy. The declassified Commanding Officer's voyage reports were used where specific dates, times, and events are entered. The names listed throughout are real people with their real names, most of whom are probably deceased by now.

One of the reasons for writing this account is to document for my family and other interested parties the role the Naval Armed Guard and the Merchant Marines played in World War II. The war could not have been won without the vital materials we delivered. America has never really recognized the efforts and sacrifices of these resolute seafarers. They are truly the "Unsung Sailors."

INTRODUCTION

Excerpts from submission by Arthur Lange, 8/25/00
United States Armed Guard World War II

The United States Navy Armed Guard was first organized during World War I when Allied and American shipping was being attacked by the enemy from surface ships and a new type of craft to warfare—the submarine. It was necessary for guns to be placed on ships and for gun crews to man them for protection. The U.S. Navy was called on to supply the crew, and they were called "Armed Guard". The World War I Armed Guard was deactivated following the end of the war, after the guns were removed. They had served on 384 ships.

The Armed Guard crew consisted of the Officers, Gunners, Radiomen, Signalmen and later on, Medics and Radarmen. They were assisted by the Army and Merchant Marine volunteers on many occasions, for their lives were at stake, too. The radiomen and signalmen were in charge of all codes and messages sent to and received aboard the ship. The Ship's Company Personnel at the Receiving Stations were almost as important as the gunners, for without them there would not have been any mail calls, clothing or good chow.

In April, 1941, with the war in Europe spreading over the boundaries of neighboring countries and another world conflict possible for the United States, measures were being taken to man the cargo ships again, because the Allies had lost many ships since 1939. Even though the Allies were having many ships sunk during the 1940-41 era, Congress could not authorize placing guns aboard cargo ships due to the 1939 Neutrality Act, Section 6. This act prohibited the arming of US Merchant vessels during the existence of the proclamation of a state of war between foreign states or countries. It was not until the Act of November 17, 1941, (55-STAT.764) Section 2 for the Neutrality Act that repealed Section 6, before steps were enacted to arm the merchant ships. Training, however, was already in progress.

On April 15, 1941, men from several Naval Reserve units received gunnery training and were then sent home. Some 100 Reserve Officers also received special gun training during the summer at the Naval Academy for possible duty on board merchant ships. On September 17, 1941, men arrived at Little Creek, Virginia, to begin gun crew training. It was a section Navy base in the swamps on U.S. Route 60, with only a mess hall, administration building, and one barrack where guns were placed out back. From this the Armed Guard grew to 144,970 personnel before the war was to end. This was more than the entire fleet of 1935. These men were the first to man the few guns that were available at that time, and it was not before October 15, 1941, that the Little Creek base officially opened.

World War II brought a different type of war than World War I. Even though submarines had been used in World War I, they were greatly improved in range and firepower. They could stay underwater longer and stalk their prey until all was in their favor. The casualty rates were high among the Armed Guard crew and Merchant Seamen due to the fact that the enemy ruled below sea with subs, on the sea with their superior ships and raiders, and above the sea with their fighters, bombers, and torpedo planes. The planes did their damage to the shipping whenever they came within range, such as from the English Channel to Russia's ports of Murmansk and Archangel. The enemy planes were a great menace in the Mediterranean Sea until the U.S. gained control.

The Merchant Marine Chairman was quoted as saying, "If it was not for the merchant shipping and seaman, the war would have been lost by the Allies." It could also be said, "If it were not for the United States Navy Armed Guard crews and the protection they provided, the ship, cargo and merchant crew lives would have been lost, and so would the war. You can be assured that it took the cooperation of all personnel of the peace loving countries, both civilian and military, doing their duty for mankind, to bring about peace and stability."

At the beginning of World War II, many merchant ships were sunk within the lights of our shorelines since the light from the cities along the coast made a silhouette of our ships as they passed between the submarines and the glow from the shore. The coast of the Carolinas soon became called "Torpedo Alley" by the crews, since the ships looked like sitting ducks in a gallery. The owners of the businesses along the Eastern Seaboard were afraid they would lose customers if the lights were cut off, and it was only after official orders that they were blacked out.

The requirement to serve in the Armed Guard was to be in good health in every respect for there were no doctors aboard. Good night vision was essential along with 20/20 vision. It was hoped that the men on watch could spot the enemy before the enemy spotted them, and that quick action could be taken to avoid contact.

Early in the war, some of the ships were caught with no guns aboard. Many of the ships' crew placed creosote poles to appear as big guns. Guns were soon installed on ships going to priority destinations. The "Lewis" machine guns were soon replaced by 20 MM and the creosote poles by modern 3"/50 and 5"/38 guns.

The U.S. Navy Armed Guard crews were a dedicated crew of men with love for their country and the people of other countries that wished to be self-governed. They soon gained respect from the enemy for their ability to perform the jobs as gunners.

Of the 6,236 merchant ships the Armed Guard served on, 710 were sunk with many damaged. Of these 2,710 were famous "Liberty Ships," with 216 sunk. Over 80,000 of the original Armed Guard were transferred into the fleet as the "Battle of the Atlantic" slowed, and experienced gun crews were needed in the Pacific Theatre of war. There was a big demand for experienced gunners on the LSTs and LCIs, for invasions that were to come. Many were placed aboard the larger ships as relief replacements.

The Armed Guard branch of service was again de-activated as soon as World War II was over, and all guns were removed. Many of the crews transferred to the regular Navy, making a career of the service until retirement. Most returned to the place from whence they came: farms, factories, schools, and service stations. They returned to the country, small towns, and big cities to be engulfed back into society, only to soon become the "Forgotten Heroes." The conflict had taken men to almost every port in the world and 1,810 to their final resting place.

Chapter 1
THE EARLY YEARS

COLD...COLD.... BONE MARROW FREEZING COLD.
I had never been so cold in my life. "Cold!" said the destroyer's captain; "It's cold enough to freeze the tail off a brass monkey!" Even when later living in Alaska for thirty-six years, I was never that cold.
There were two periods in my life when I experienced that kind of cold. The first was during the spring of 1942 while serving as a Naval Armed Guard gunner on board the SS Eldena, a Merchant ship in a convoy transporting war materials to Murmansk, Russia, known as the Murmansk Run.
The second was in February 1943, in a Navy torpedo bomber in which I was flying as turret gunner. It crash landed in the Atlantic Ocean just off Long Island, New York. Long Island Sound was frozen over at the time.
But then I am getting ahead of myself. Maybe I should start at the beginning.

* * *

I was born May 1st, 1923, near Lincolnton, Georgia, the son of John Ira Haynes and Lecia Mae McDonald. There were also two daughters, Carmen E. whom we called "Jean" and Lecia G. whom we called by her initials, "L.G." My mother often called me "Sammie" because she said that I was an answer to her prayer. She dedicated me to the Lord as in the Bible story of Hannah in 1 Samuel, Chapter 1.

During all my early years until I went into the Navy, all family and friends used my middle name, "Lanier", but the Navy used first name, middle initial, so thereafter it has been "John".

My father, Ira, whom we later called "Pop" was a sawyer/farmer and at the time we lived in a sawmill shack at Soap Creek (now under water due to a hydroelectric reservoir on the Savannah River). Harvesting timber in the Georgia/ South Carolina area required moving to where the timber was located; as a result, the family often lived in quick-built shacks nearby. By the time I was school age we lived on and worked a small farm near Appling, Georgia, while Pop still worked as a sawyer during the Depression years.

I guess we were poor by some standards, but as children we didn't know it. We always had food, sometimes sparse, but I don't ever remember going hungry. We had adequate clothes, but not a lot. If I got a new pair of bib overalls, I wore them until the knees gave out, then wore them as cut-offs. The cut-off parts were saved for patches. My parents were very frugal.

Growing up I had no Tinker-Toys, Erector sets or Leggos. It is surprising how much fun a kid can have with a spool and a piece of string. I made my own toys. My gun for playing Cowboys was a piece of L-shaped wood with a clothes pin on the butt end to which I attached a piece of inner-tube rubber band stretched to the front of the barrel. Releasing it would sting the "bad guy" and "Bang, you're dead!" I also made pop-guns from sections of elderberry with the center pith removed and a ram rod to shoot green china berries. I always got high praise from Mom for all my accomplishments; she made me feel like I could do anything. I even built my own crude bed from rough sawn lumber and Mom let me put it in my room. I slept on it for several years.

Pop's timber business began to prosper a bit and he bought and operated his own portable sawmill. It was powered by a big gasoline motor and connected to the mill by wide flat drive belts which operated the big circle saw, the log carriage, the edger and a long drag chain to pull the sawdust from under the saw. He had a huge Belgium horse named Prince that he used for snaking logs in the woods. I loved to ride on him when I went to the mill with Pop.

Christmas of 1934 was the best ever for the family. The girls got a piano and I got a beautiful paint pony that I named "Pet". With our border collie "Jeff" I would ride Pet through the pasture and round up the cows for the evening. Sometimes I'd ride a few miles to visit my best friend, Lester Tankersley, who had a new bicycle, and we would exchange rides. I didn't own a bicycle until several years later. Sadly Lester drowned in a pond behind their home in 1947.

In the summer of 1935 the family moved to Augusta, Georgia, where I completed the sixth and seventh grades and then went to the Academy of Richmond County, a Junior ROTC Military High School, graduating in 1941. In 1940 I joined the Marine Corps Reserves for about a year, and during the summer that year went on active duty for two weeks training at the Marine Base at Quantico, Virginia. I worked at Sears in the display and shoe departments part-time while going to school and full-time after graduation.

During those years I was active in the Boy Scouts and spent as much time as possible around the Augusta airport. I loved to watch the light planes fly and see the airliners come and go. I was at the airport the day Delta Airlines landed with its first big new Douglas DC-3. It was awe-inspiring.

I wanted to fly. I built and flew model airplanes as Scouting projects. One such project was a flying model of the Fairchild 22 with a 22" wing span. After completing and flying it successfully with its rubber band powered propeller, I decided to build a much larger model. I took all the measurements and multiplied by a factor of three, which gave me a wing span of 5 ½ feet. Built exactly to scale, it was quite an impressive airplane. It was, however, much heavier and I had no proper means of propulsion. Rubber bands were out of the question and other means were not available to me at the time. I even drew a fantasy design for a "Buck Rogers" style one-man, strap-on vertical take-off machine which I thought, at the time, might work.... I really did want to be a pilot. My first airplane ride was in a Ford Tri-Motor on a sight-seeing ride over the city.

Hunting was my other passion. I hunted Bob White quail with Pop and my uncle Fred McDonald. I learned a lot from them about wing shooting, angle of flight, target lead and speed estimation. Pop was a very good bird shot and would usually get two or three out of a flushed covey. Uncle Fred was deadly, dropping five birds out of five shots from his Browning Auto 12 gauge, and sometimes two birds with one shot. My other favorite game was waterfowl. I hunted ducks on the Savannah River, many times alone, if I could find no one to hunt with me. Fast flying

Mallards, Green Wing Teal, Red Head and Ring Neck ducks over decoys or pass shooting tends to hone the skills. There was no big game such as white tail deer in that part of Georgia when I was growing up. Happily I got the opportunity for wonderful big game hunting in Alaska many years later.

Chapter 2
WORLD WAR II BEGINS

On December 7, 1941, after Pearl Harbor was bombed by Japan the United States declared war and World War II began. As President Roosevelt said, it was "a day that shall live in infamy". It was the day of great change for my life and the lives of many other Americans. On December 8th, my cousin Herman McDonald and I, along with several others who worked at Sears, volunteered for Military service. Bill Ready, George Chavous, Herman, and I joined the Navy, while others went into other branches. I tried to sign up for flight training to be a Navy Pilot. The recruiter said I needed two years of college to qualify. I had just graduated from high-school six months earlier, so that squelched that. He said, however, that there was a possibility of getting flight training as an enlisted pilot, Naval Aviation Pilots (NAP), but I would have to join the Regular Navy, that is USN instead of the Reserve, USNR. If there was a chance, I wanted to go for it. I signed up for Regular Navy six-year enlistment.

One week later, on December 15th, we traveled by rail to Macon, Georgia, to be sworn in, and thence to the Naval Operating Base at Norfolk, Virginia, for boot camp. Boot Camp was 3 ½ weeks of intensive training that included inspections, drills, signal flags, rifle qualification, swimming, life boat operation and many other things. We had an "Old Salt", Chief Petty Officer Liptrap, as our commanding officer. He had an arm full of service stripes "Hash Marks" on his sleeve, and was probably recalled to active duty from retirement. He had to be treated as a commissioned officer, saluted, "Sir" and "Yes, Sir" during our training.

He was a great CO, strict, considerate, fair and was well-liked and respected.

During the training we were allowed to indicate a preference of trade schools or specialties. Having been bitten by the lore of aviation early in life and wanting to qualify for the NAP program, I applied for all the aviation specialties.

I wrote home: *"If I don't make school, I can get a transfer to an aircraft carrier and apply for school after about a month."* Wishful thinking…this was not to be.

A large number of us were assigned to the Naval Armed Guard and sent for further training at Little Creek, Virginia. To be selected for the Armed Guard a sailor needed to be physically fit with excellent eye sight, especially good night vision. There were no doctors, corpsmen, or medical facilities on merchant ships.

Little Creek was a small ill-equipped camp hastily set up to provide gunnery training for Naval Armed Guard. Training for these new raw recruits, many of whom had never seen a ship and some had never seen the ocean, was no easy task. There was a shortage of everything—most of all guns. What heavy weapons were available at the training center were mostly for show. There was very little formal Navy education in the early stages, and one brand-new gunnery officer was told on his introduction to guns, "This is a 4-inch gun and this is a 3-inch gun, and if you don't believe it, you can get a ruler and measure it."

The situation was repeated in many areas. At Little Creek, there were three tired old gunships used for training: the USS *Paducah*, USS *Dubuque*, and the USS *Eagle*. Live gunnery practice, however, consisted of only one day "at sea," in Chesapeake Bay, observing gunnery drills and luckily getting to fire one round. I was on the USS *Paducah* (Gunboat No. 18) which was launched in 1904 and served during World War II to train Armed Guard gunners in Chesapeake Bay.

Back at Little Creek camp we were given a bit more training on the .50-caliber machine guns mounted on pedestals with bicycle type handle bars and iron sights for aiming the guns. They had canisters that held 50 rounds requiring a second person as loader during operation. There were also WW-1 vintage .30-caliber Lewis machine guns which held its rounds in a pan attached to the top of the gun. The training consisted of safety precautions, disassembling and assembling, cleaning and maintenance. The actual firing of the weapons was done at stationary targets, sleds towed by boats just off shore and at target sleeves towed behind aircraft.

On January 22nd 1942, we were shipped to the Armed Guard Center at Brooklyn, New York. This center was responsible for records, mail, and pay accounts, as well as for issuing proper clothing and many other details. The AG Center was the AG's wartime duty station when not assigned to a ship. It was a very large building near the harbor that resembled a blimp hangar.

Inside was a large chow hall and bunk beds stacked five and six bunks high. I always chose the top bunk. I didn't like guys climbing over me. I had become friends with one of the crew, Paul Harkey, who bunked just below me. We were here only two days before being assigned to a ship. **At this time I had been the Navy less than 6 weeks!**

Chapter 3
THE VOYAGE BEGINS

Our Gun Crew was assigned to the SS *Eldena*. She was a 459 foot, 6900 ton, "Flush Deck" freighter that was built in 1919 and was operated by the Robin Lines of Seattle until she was taken over by the U. S. Maritime Commission January 2, 1942. She was sent to New Jersey for degaussing, the purpose of which was to try to neutralize the ships magnetic field, thus making it less susceptible to attracting magnetic mines and to lessen the magnetic deviation of the ships compass. On Jan. 19th she moved over to Bethlehem Steel in Brooklyn for installation of gun foundations, splinter protection, fire control com systems, darkening ship facilities and painting.

Her armament to be operated by the Armed Guard was:

One 4"/50 caliber World War 1 cannon mounted on the stern.

Two .50-caliber Browning machine guns aft of the bridge deck port and starboard.

Two .50-caliber Browning machine guns forward of the poop deck port and starboard.

Two .30-caliber Lewis WW-1 machine guns on the wing of the bridge port and starboard.

Two .30-caliber Lewis WW-1 machine guns on the boat deck aft port and starboard.

The .50-caliber Browning guns were pedestal mounted in 4' high, ½" thick steel tubs about 14' in diameter raised 8' above the deck like a mushroom and accessed by a steel ladder. My battle station was as gunner in the starboard tub aft of the bridge.

Armed Guard quarters were provided: For the Officer in Charge a room under the bridge. For the Petty Officers and seamen, eight bunks starboard side, main deck aft; 4 bunks port side, main deck aft; and 4 bunks under the fo'c's'le forward. Paul Harkey and I, along with two other AGs were in the cabin under the fo'c's'le.

January 24th part of the gun crew reported aboard the Eldena consisting of:

Officer in Charge: FINK, Frederick S. Ensign USNR
Enlisted men:
SHIPLEY, Francis M. Cox USN
HARKEY, Paul Koenig AS USNR
HAYNES, John Lanier AS USN
JONES, Cole Junior AS USNR
KELLY, Ben Joseph AS USNR
LATIMER, Robert Sidney AS USN
McGRATH, Timothy F. AS USNR
MANOR, Ralph AS USN

February 4th in Boston two more were added:
DUNN, Denis Anthony Sea 1c USN
NOWLIN, Charles Leo Sea 2c USN

February 11th two more completes the crew.
CONNEL, Mathew Taylor RM 2c USNR
SARGENT, John Frederick SM 3c USNR

All of the AS (Apprentice Seaman) were green recruits, fresh out of boot camp at Norfolk, all seventeen and eighteen years old.

The Ship's Merchant Crew consisted of: Captain Ole M. Nielsen, Master, plus 36 Officers and men. A list of all of the Merchant crew with name, rank, age and country of origin will be shown in an appendix at the end of this account.

I wrote home: *"Mom, this about the biggest freighter I've ever seen or heard of. She sits so far up out of the water it's like looking down at the water from a skyscraper."* The ship was empty at the time.

January 29th the *Eldena* departed New York, arriving in Boston on the 31st. For the next ten days tons of war materials were loaded in her holds. Food stuffs, clothing, grain, tires, spare parts for trucks, tanks and aircraft, weapons, munitions, high explosives, drums of high-octane gasoline and more filled the holds. That being done and the hatches battened down, the above deck was loaded with trucks and crated airplanes. The crowded deck left little room for moving from one end of the ship to the other. This was especially troublesome in rough sea and icing conditions.

My last letter home before the voyage began: *"It is plenty cold here in Boston. It has been snowing for the past two days; you can hardly see the ship for the snow and ice. Before it started snowing, it was so cold that you could spit on the deck but before it hit the deck it would freeze and bounce. We tried to paint the guns but the paint froze on the guns, on the brushes, and in the bucket. We haven't been able to paint them yet. This will be my last letter for probably six months, so don't worry."*

By February 11th we were underway to Halifax, Nova Scotia, where we were to join other ships for the outbound convoy crossing the Atlantic. This was our first real chance to check our guns and test fire them. All guns operated satisfactorily at the time. Even though it was rather cold in these latitudes, we stood watches in our battle station tubs four hours on and four hours off.

February 16th...**I had been in the Navy for 2 months now**...Convoy SC-70 formed and cleared to get underway. The first ship out at 1021 was the American freighter SS *Eldena*. Our position in the convoy was right in the center, 4th column, 2nd row, i.e. #42.

The distance to Scotland is some 2500 miles and the convoy could go only as fast as the slowest ship, 5.8 knots. One of our poor guys, Tim McGrath, would get seasick just looking at a ship. He would be sick for days. The merchant crew had lots of fun with him. They would suggest all kinds of remedies, one of which was eating greasy fat pork. He would try this and then head for the rails to feed the fish. Luckily I was never seasick even in the roughest of seas.

The Merchant Marines on the *Eldena* were generally older experienced seamen. Captain Nielsen was a 56 year-old Norwegian-American; the 2nd Mate, Lee was 62; Chief Engineer Bain was Scottish 58; and the Steward, Lucas, was 55. The youngest was the Radio Operator, Fhelps, 19, with all the rest somewhere in between.

There were times of friction between the Merchant Marines and the Armed Guard and it took a while for these to settle down. A former merchant seaman turned exceptional author stated that the merchant marine attracted the adventurer, the homeless, the restless, and included the emotionally unstable, alcoholics, or just plain hard cases who loved trouble. Many were tough characters, termed "performers," veterans of bitter union-organizing strife, and more familiar with bars, brothels, and brawls than in cultural pursuit in worldwide ports. They jeered at the "Sea Scouts," who had never been on, or perhaps even seen, a ship before. They also resented sharing quarters with newcomers who had to be jammed into already cramped space. They laughed at the discipline and low pay of the navy gun crews and the "landlubbers" who commanded them.

On the other hand, a favorite jibe of the AGs was, "There are only three kinds of time aboard ship: sack time, coffee time and overtime." There were also some unkind references to "high-paid draft dodgers." Needling included such things as, "If you're really in the Navy why aren't you on a Navy ship?" Answers could be unprintable. The merchant crew was constantly, 'riding' the Navy crew; telling them they were suckers for working for such small pay, that they didn't have to obey their officer, as they were not 'real' Navy men, but just civilians drafted into service.[1]

These examples were not prevalent on the *Eldena*. We soon became friends and shipmates, especially after we had our first encounter with the enemy. "Sharing their lives and their deaths were their shipmates, the officers and men of the merchant marine, who proved time and again that heroism and devotion to country are not restricted to any one body of men. They manned and maneuvered the ships under attack, passed ammunition and fought at the guns alongside often-understrength or incapacitated navy gun crews."[2]

March 6th we arrived in Scotland and anchored in the *Firth of Clyde* near Greenock, some eighty miles west of Glasgow. It was beautiful with its snow covered rolling mountains. The next day we moved a short distance and anchored again in *Loch Long*, then on the 8th we were underway again, this time for *Loch Ewe* where we would form Convoy PQ-13 destined for Murmansk. We were not allowed to go ashore at all in Scotland...we felt cheated.

Note; Fifty-four years later my wife, Juanita, and I visited Scotland celebrating our 50th wedding anniversary. Our bus tour took us from Glasgow along the Firth of Clyde and Loch Long and north to Loch Ewe where the WWII convoys were formed.

Chapter 4
CONVOY PQ-13

March 10th at 1515 Convoy PQ-13 got underway from *Loch Ewe* to Reykjavik, Iceland, 842 miles distant. This leg of the voyage was uneventful and sort of pleasant except for the cold. Remember I was a thin-blooded Georgia boy, who until this voyage had never experienced cold weather. Where I grew up there was the occasional freeze or freezing rain or even a ½" of snow some years, but seldom enough to build even a small snowman. The cold penetrated to the bone. I would put on as many layers of clothes as I could find in my sea bag.

The Convoy Cruising Order is designated by column and row. PQ-13 was organized in this manner:

#11 *Dunboyne*, #21 *Harpalion*, #31 *Empire Cowper*, #41 *Induna*, #51 *River Afton*, #61 *Tobruk*,

#12 *Effingham*, #22 *Empire Starlight*, #32 *Empire Ranger*, #42 *Raceland*, #52 *New Westminster City*, #62 *Gallant Fox*,

#13 *Eldena*, #23 *Mormacmar*, #33 *Mana*, #43 *Lars Kruse*, #53 *El Estero*, #63 *Mano*.

Thus, our ship *Eldena*, the first ship of the last row was considered the "coffin corner".

March 15th we anchored in Reykjavik harbor for three days, but again we were not allowed to go ashore. On this date I had been in the Navy for three months. In addition to the Convoy PQ-13 Cruising Order shown, the Panamanian ship, SS *Bateau* and the British *Scottish American* also took part, both joining off Iceland (stations not known). Also the Panamanian, SS *Ballot* joined up on March 26.

March 18th 0645, Convoy PQ-13 sailed from Reykjavik with the Commodore in *River Afton* and the Vice Commodore in *Induna*. The convoy later returned towards Iceland, having heard the news that the German battleship, *Tirpitz* had left Norway, but the convoy later turned around toward Murmansk again. According to *Induna*'s report, they left Reykjavik on March 20. Convoy speed: 6.2 knots.

During the next few days we had to be especially alert on watch from our gun tubs. We had entered a huge floating mine field laid out by the enemy U-boat Wolf-Pack. We spotted and maneuvered around these floating killers until clear of the mine fields.

On March 23rd, to avoid dangerous areas, the course was altered to latitude 0.5 west with instructions to keep as far to the northeast as ice conditions would permit. With the close proximity of the polar ice the temperature dropped as low as 40°F below zero. It became a constant battle to clear ice and snow off the deck and superstructure. Mast stays assumed gigantic proportions as ice encased them six to eight inches thick, and they had to be attacked with sledge hammers to free them of ice. The ship itself was grinding through pack ice with a growling, cracking noise.

March 25th, the weather deteriorated rapidly, and a ferocious gale blew up from the Northeast, roaring down from the North Pole. This was no ordinary gale; this was the mother and father of all gales. The deeply laden ships pitched and rolled in the mountainous seas, and would sink into the valleys of enormous waves with just their topmasts visible. Then the tortuous climb to the next wave pinnacle revealed their salt-encrusted, scarified hulls with racing propellers before falling with a shuddering crash into the next trough. Thunderous seas poured over and down the decks, finding way into ventilators and cabins.

To open a door at the wrong moment was to invite a flooded cabin. Regular hot meals were out of the question; we existed on coffee and sandwiches. Even this had to be brought from the galley and was a death-defying act. One waited until the ship gained some sort of equilibrium and then made a mad dash across the deck. With any luck you might make it without getting soaked. The difficult part was returning with a can of coffee and sandwiches in one hand and still keeping a hold on the lifeline.[3]

It was during one of these acrobatic roll and pitches on a particularly high wave that one of our AGs, Tim McGrath, stepped out of the cabin onto the deck to go on watch. The ship had just dived into an oncoming swell and was rising out of it sending a torrent of water cascading down the deck from bow to stern, sweeping Tim off his feet. He went careening aft on his back, feet and arms flailing in attempt to grab something. As the ship rose over that one she took on a load of water over the stern, sending Tim back toward the bow. It is doubtful that he would have survived had he not been grabbed by a shipmate just as he was going past.

Lifelines had been strung fore and aft on both sides of the ship, but it was extremely dangerous for us to try to get from the galley to our quarters in the fo'c's'le. Gun station watches were suspended during the storm.

Mills writes "The noise of the wind was indescribable; howling and screaming like a banshee. The air laden with flying spume froze as it struck the ship, turning it into a white, ghostly, spectra laboring through this hellish frozen world. Watch-keepers and gunners rapidly became ice-sculptured silhouettes, moving lethargically. The warm air they breathed out immediately froze into tiny icicles around the slits of their headgear. Eyelids were constantly brushed to stop them freezing together; hairs in the nostrils became icicles that pierced the nose when rubbed. Only later, after thawing out, one felt the pain.

The convoy had scattered during this ferocious gale which lasted more than forty-eight hours. It was a horrendous experience; we were continually soaked to the skin, frozen to the marrow, half-starved from lack of hot food, physically exhausted from the sheer effort of trying to stay upright. The screaming wind from the North Pole tore the tops of forty to fifty foot waves, filling the air with flying spray that hit one like frozen bullets.

It was awesome to see the ship drive into, and under, these gigantic waves then, slowly, agonizingly, shuddering like a trapped animal, struggle to lift her head from under the colossal weight of water. Huge seas cascaded over her fo'c's'le and poured down the length of the ship. At times I really thought we had been overwhelmed and were sinking. We were reaching the limits of physical endurance when the gale moderated."[4]

When it began to subside a bit we found ourselves in heavy ice floe. Huge flat ice chunks 25 to 100 feet in diameter jammed together looking like scales on a gigantic sea monster that appeared to breath as the swells rose and fell. Pack ice could do severe damage to the ship's hull. The grinding and scraping noise as we ploughed through was nerve-racking.

March 27th we were joined by four ships from the convoy, all of us still in the ice floe. We were safer here from U-boats, but were vulnerable to air attack since we were now within range of the German aircraft, strung out in many bases along the Norwegian coast. The Germans basically used five types of aircraft to attack shipping: Dorniers (high-level bombing), Heinkels (torpedo bombers), Stukers (dive bombers), Focke-Wulf 200s (bombers and long distance reconnaissance) and Blohm-Voss (bombers).

"It's arrived." No explanation was necessary. We knew that forerunner of evil, a long-range reconnaissance plane, was circling the convoy reporting our every movement. They always circled just out of gun range. On one occasion a destroyer signaled the plane, "You're making me dizzy, would you mind going around the other way." To which the German pilot immediately obliged, proving he had a sense of humor.

Chapter 5
JIG HOW

March 28th we were joined by two more merchant ships from the convoy, the destroyer HMS *Eclipse* and two trawlers. We were easing out of the field ice but in intermittent snow showers and fog. The visibility ranged from 200 yards to a half-mile with breaks in the clouds through which we caught glimpse of the reconnaissance plane. Not long after, an unidentifiable bomber was seen through the cloud breaks approaching the convoy. Our signalmen, John Sargent "Flags", spotted a flag hoist go up on the Commodore's ship.

The signal was unmistakable, a signal he had memorized from the Mersigs Code Book. It was "Jig How," which meant *"Man your guns and prepare for instant action."* He relayed the message to Captain Nielsen, who instantly pressed the General Quarters Alarm. ("Jig How" was the phonetic pronunciation of the alphabet flags J and H.)[5]

We were already at our battle stations when the bomber came within range. I was in the starboard tub aft of the bridge along with my loader, Ralph Manor. I got off two .50-caliber rounds and my gun jammed. The other three .50s had the same problem to varying degrees, and we were out of action at a critical time. The lubricant on the action had frozen and would not recoil to eject the spent case and load another round. This was our first encounter with the enemy and we were unable to respond. We stripped the guns down and tried to clean the action with solvent in a bucket while on station in the gun tubs, but our hands were freezing and there was ice forming in the bucket.

Our C.O., Ensign Fink, ordered us to bring the guns into the galley area and get warm before trying to clean them again. With the solvent heated and our hands warmed, we thoroughly cleaned and reassembled them without any lubrication whatever. This worked so well that we did not use any lube during the entire voyage.

At 1438, Radioman, Matt Connell "Sparks", received a distress message from the *Empire Ranger*, being bombed by aircraft. Again at 1818, "*Empire Ranger* sinking. Am abandoning ship and heading for the coast". Also at 1438 the *Harpalion* was bombed but was able to continue to Murmansk.

The SS *Raceland* had lost contact with the convoy due to heavy weather and equipment malfunction. That day, the German bombers attacked the ship. The aircraft came right above them, but disappeared again; a few shots were exchanged. The next time the aircraft came from behind. Again the alarm sounded; all men got their lifebelts. The ship was poorly equipped in the way of defense, (there was no Armed Guard aboard) and the aircraft dropped two bombs from about 30 meters. They went underneath the ship and destroyed the slabs and plating in the engine room on the port side, so that the ship immediately started to list to starboard at a sharp angle.

At 10:30 that evening *Raceland* went down. A tall column of flames went to the skies in the tremendous explosion that followed. In the middle of the fire the profile of a raft being flung to the skies could be seen. And then, finally, the lifeboats tried to set a course for Murmansk. All four were tied together, and the 2nd mate, who had a good compass, was the leader. They had about 600 miles to go.

A day later a storm and a freezing cold caused two lifeboats to sink with twelve crewmembers on board. The boats were separated and never saw each other again. This weather lasted for the eleven days they were on the sea. The other two lifeboats reached land, and due to the suffering only 13 crewmembers of the 45 survived.[6]

Unknown to us three German Narvik destroyers, Z24, Z25 and Z26 had steamed from their base in Kirkenes, Norway to attack the convoy. About 2240 they spotted the *Bateau*, torpedoed and sunk her.

Back at my battle station in the gun tub, from my high position, I had a clear view of our small convoy rising and falling in a moderate sea. The sky was overcast and there were frequent snow squalls. Efforts to keep warm by flapping arms and stamping feet were arrested by the sound of heavy gunfire. A dull glow occasionally lit up the horizon.

We knew we were sailing into a naval battle but at that young stage of my life I had no concept of fear. Our gallant destroyers, one of which was an old "four-stacker" laid a heavy smoke screen around the convoy and with the oncoming darkness, due to short daylight hours in that latitude, we were spared the surface battle for a few hours.

On March 29th the convoy was joined by the Battle Cruiser HMS *Trinidad* and Destroyers HMS *Fury*, HMS *Eclipse* and HMS *Paynter*. Then at 0930, hull down on the horizon on the port side of the convoy were the silhouettes of the three German destroyers as they raced out of a snow squall. There were gun flashes followed by the rumbling whine of shells as they passed overhead to explode harmlessly in the sea. Two shells hit with splashes astern of the ship ahead in the column on the port side, four splashes just astern of the ship ahead, one about a hundred yards dead ahead of the *Eldena*. One shell exploded about 75 yards directly off our port beam amidships and three more just astern of the ship in the next column to port. Several shells were heard passing overhead or close by.[7]

The *Trinidad* and the destroyers raced to engage the enemy entering a heavy snow squall. During this time heavy gunfire could be heard going from the port bow of the convoy to the port beam. In a break in the snow squall we could see one German ship had already been badly hit and was on fire astern. Within seconds they vanished into another bank of snow. It was like a dream sequence. We could hardly believe what we had seen. "The reality of the situation became apparent some thirty minutes later when emerging from a snow storm we came upon the cruiser HMS *Trinidad*, lying dead in the water with a huge hole in her side from which smoke and flames poured. There was great consternation as we viewed the stricken ship. How was it possible the smaller German ships had beaten this powerful ship? Only later did we learn that by a million to one chance, she had torpedoed herself. Apparently, one of her own torpedoes had malfunctioned—possibly a frozen gyro—had run wild in a circle, striking the *Trinidad*. Slowly we steamed past the stricken cruiser with her attendant destroyers to ward off any U-boats.

We left the *Trinidad* in what appeared to be a sinking condition. Heeled over, shrouded in smoke and flames, she looked like a doomed ship. In fact, the crew managed to contain the fires and get the engines started, and she made Murmansk before we arrived. With the absence of the cruiser and her attendant destroyers we felt naked and undefended, especially as we were approaching the most dangerous part of the voyage—the Kola Inlet. A line of U-boats lay across our path and German bombers were barely fifty flying miles away. Here was our most vulnerable point."[8]

Although appearing badly hit, the *Trinidad* was making way under her own power and did, in fact, reach Murmansk safely where she underwent temporary repairs. The convoy continued with no change of course or speed, encountering heavy field ice throughout the night. The approximate position of the attack was 72°07'N/32°15'E.

March 30th at 0620 we received a radio message from the British ship, *Induna*, with the Vice-Commodore aboard. A straggler from the convoy due to bad weather, she was hit by one of three torpedoes from U-376 and caught fire northeast of the Kola Inlet. The ship was hit aft by a coup-de-grâce at 0932, but only sank by the bow after being missed by a second coup-de-grâce at 0940. The U-boat did not question the survivors because a periscope had been sighted. Unknown to them it was U-209 which had chased the same ship after missing it with a spread of two torpedoes at 0552.

In the meantime, on 28 March, the Panamanian steam merchant *Ballot*, a ship of this group, was bombed and damaged by a German aircraft at 72°40N/27°35E. Sixteen men abandoned ship in a lifeboat for unknown reasons. According to the master they had demanded to leave *Ballot*, while the remaining crew stayed to repair the ship and brought her safely to Murmansk on 30 March. The men in the lifeboat were picked up by the escorting armed trawler, and later transferred to *Induna*. These two ships got stuck in ice the next day, after the group headed north to evade the U-boats reported in the area.

The other ships of the group continued to Murmansk, while the crews worked several hours to free the vessels from the ice and the *Induna* then took HMS *Silja* (FY 301) in tow because she was low on fuel. The next night the tow parted in heavy seas and they were unable to find the trawler in snow squalls, so *Induna* continued alone until being torpedoed by U-376.

Forty-one survivors abandoned ship in two lifeboats, but when they were picked up by a Russian minesweeper on 2 April, only thirty were still alive and two of them later died of exposure in a hospital in Murmansk.

The weather had been horrible with temperatures around 20° below zero and freezing winds. The survivors were sprayed by ice cold water and most of them lost limbs. The master, 20 crew members, 6 gunners and 11 men from *Ballot* were lost. 19 crew members, 4 gunners and 5 men from *Ballot* survived.[9]

Note: One of the survivors was Engineer Officer, William Short, of Scotland, who wrote an article in the May 2005 issue of the POINTER telling of his ordeal and hospital stay in Murmansk. After reading his story, I wrote to him in 2009, but did not receive an answer.

On March 29th our sister ship, the *Effingham*, lost contact with the convoy PQ-13 in the Barents Sea after an attack by the three German destroyers Z-24, Z-25 and Z-26 and tried to proceed alone about ninety miles behind the convoy.

The ship caught fire, and after two hours the fire reached the cargo, causing the ship to explode. The master, the chief mate, and fifteen men in the first lifeboat were picked up by the HMS *Harrier* (N 71), but six men had died of exposure. Sixty-five hours after the attack, eleven men and three of the armed guards in the other boat were picked up by a Soviet patrol boat, but four men had also died of exposure. In all eleven crewmen and one armed guard died. The survivors were all taken to Murmansk, where they lived on various merchant ships until they were repatriated. Six of them returned to the US on the *Eldena* in convoy QP-11.

0745 on the 30th the Commodore in *River Afton* sent a visual message that a submarine was sighted bearing 063° true but out of range, so we never saw him. 0835 a radio report that *Mana* was torpedoed but gave no position. Two Russian destroyers, the *Gremyashchi* and *Sokrushitelny*, reinforced us. Fleet Minesweepers *Gossamer*, *Harrier* and *Speedwell*, also joined us and began circling the convoy, dropping depth charges to keep down submarines. At 1430 the SS *Mana* joined the convoy from the starboard bow. At 1500 another sister ship, the SS *Dunboyne* (Ernest Prahter, Master) joined the convoy from the starboard side.

Note: The first Armed Guard crew #1E of WWII (seven men under a coxswain) went aboard the Liberty ship S.S. Dunboyne on December 2, 1941. Before sailing four more were added, including the CO, Ensign Rufus Brinn.

Earlier a storm broke up the convoy and left their ship and five others with only a trawler for escort. A scout bomber attacked on the morning of March 28, but dropped its bombs into the sea after the *Dunboyne* opened fire with all nine of her guns.

Later in the day a bomber dropped five bombs close to the SS *Mana* and five close to the SS *Ballot*. The *Ballot* developed trouble with her steering gear and dropped astern out of sight. They kept together for six days and finally made rendezvous with the balance of the convoy, only to find that the escorting cruiser had been ordered to leave for another more important assignment.

The convoy proceeded to Murmansk by a far northern route, taking advantage of the midwinter all-day darkness of Arctic waters. As they approached their destination, they became stuck in the ice of the Barents Sea, with the temperature 40° below zero. Three of the ships were able to break out; German planes destroyed the other two; and a submarine torpedoed one of the remaining three. It was April when the last two fought off ice and the enemy and went into Murmansk.

Chapter 6
MURMANSK

March 30th, we were approaching the mouth of the Kola Inlet with the convoy in single file. Only nine of the original twenty vessels were present when the entry was made into the port of Murmansk. Already, we could smell Mother Russia, the pungent odor of forests, sawn timber, and that indefinable earthy mustiness. Even the entry into port was contested by the Germans. When the convoy was abeam Kildin Island, about twenty miles north of Murmansk, about four bombs were dropped ahead of the *Eldena* and two near the *Mormacmar*. One of the bombs damaged the *Mormacmar* slightly. Enemy submarines were also in the area and were heavily attacked by the escorting vessels. The presence of Russian planes and the effective fire from anti-aircraft guns in the hills around Murmansk were welcome sights to the battle-weary men as their ships slipped through Kola Inlet and came to anchor at Murmansk.

The sea was moderate with low patchy cloud. The enemy tactics were different than previous attacks when they had swept in low over sea level. This time they remained above cloud level, diving through the breaks. "Concentrate on the holes in the clouds", shouted our CO, Ens. Fink. Over on the starboard side I saw the Polish ship *Tobruk* being attacked. She put up a fierce defense, and even claimed a bomber shot down. Shore batteries and destroyers opened fire as well as the merchant ships.

Then it was our turn as a Junker JU 88 dived through the cloud straight for us. Every gun on the ship opened up with a roar. The sky was full of tracer bullets and flack from AA guns. It looked like a New Year's Day celebration. Here was my moment of glory; I was eyeball to eyeball with a German bomber. The thing filled my gun sight; I could see its cannons firing along its wings. I saw the bomb leave the plane, wobble then straighten up. I don't know how many, if any, hits I scored but he did not go down. RATS!!![10]

The Nazi Luftwaffe planes were believed to be Heinkel HE111s and Junkers JU88s. Also in the mix were the screaming dive bombers, Junkers JU87s "Stuka".

At 2130 on March 30, 1942, we received the "All Clear" and anchored in the harbor at Murmansk, Russia. Only nine of the original twenty vessels were present when the entry was made into the port of Murmansk. We felt a sense of relief..."We made it." It was Easter Sunday. This euphoria was short lived, however.

Murmansk is an ice-free port in the northern most section of Russia and is accessible by road, rail, air and sea. The city and harbor are situated in a bowl surrounded by mountains and only about thirty-five miles from German airfields in Norway and Finland. Air raids were a constant menace and it was bombed daily in attempt to curb the flow of war materials to the Russian military. The planes would come swooping over the hills dropping down to water level; sweeping across the large expanse of the Inlet, criss-crossing with shells and tracers before dropping their bombs and lifting up and away over the hills.

The town, itself, was in shambles. The wooden structure of so many buildings and almost all the quays rendered large areas of the town only too susceptible to incendiary attack. Owing to the unreliability of cement in Arctic conditions, many larger buildings were in a terrible state; some simply collapsed from the shock of near misses. The Northern end of the town appeared to have been completely demolished. Of the remainder; approximately one-third was unfit for habitation. Not a single building had glass; the windows were boarded up. A heavy pall of smoke continually hung over the town. I was surprised to see a windowless shop with an appetizing display of hams, sausages and fish—all made of wood. Psychologically, I failed to understand how that display helped the starving population's morale! Crude war posters depicting the gallant Red Army soldiers were everywhere, while martial music blared out of a speaker attached to buildings and suspended from poles.

The only entertainment for the visiting sailors was the International Sailors Club; here one could get a meal—of sorts, an occasional film, and dance. The entertainment was strictly organized by the Russians who provided English-speaking hostesses. We were strongly advised that the hostesses were probably KGB Agents and to be guarded in our conversation.[11]

April 1st the *Eldena* moved to the dock to off load our deck cargo. Our sister ship, the *Dunboyne*, moored directly ahead of us. No sooner were we tied up than a squad of armed soldiers came aboard and stationed themselves around the ship. We could not fail to notice the two sentries posted on the gangway. "A Soviet officer came aboard and talked with the captain and the AG officer. He gave them a set of orders for the Americans. When posted we and our shipmates wondered if this was a friendly nation.

We quickly learned there were only two places Americans could go; everything else was out of bounds. The two were the International Club and the Intourist Hotel. There was to be no contact with women, we were to speak only to hotel employees. The Americans were to be back on their ships by 10:00 pm; anyone on shore after that would be arrested and out of the ship's jurisdiction. No drunkenness was to be tolerated. There was to be no trade with civilians; it was a serious offense and could mean a jail term. If anyone got into trouble ashore, their AG officer could not help them.

As one crewmember put it 'God, what a place this is!' It didn't improve as time went by. At the Intourist Hotel an upstairs room was supposed to be a restaurant for seamen from various ships, but only tea, vodka, and a hunk of black bread was available."[12]

Working conditions onboard ship was atrocious. It was winter and the sun never rose above the horizon. There was a brief period of twilight midday, but this was often obscured by snow blizzards. Artificial light was necessary to work the cargo in the holds, but this was kept to a minimum for fear of constant air raids. Machinery had to be constantly watched and warmed through with steam pipes to prevent it freezing. Gloves could only be removed for short spells, so the simplest task such as screwing a shackle bolt into a cargo sling, or passing a wire strop assumed Herculean proportions. We were berthed at a dock which was timber floored, with a single rail track on which ran a small crane. Its lifting capacity was totally inadequate for our tanks and the crew had to jury-rig a system with our derricks. It was a very antiquated and unsafe method, but we just had to improvise. The large warehouse directly opposite the ship was already full, so our cargo was landed on the dock, where it was quickly buried in snow.

Each morning we witnessed the pathetic sight of emaciated prison labor—mostly women—being marched down to unload the ship. They were grossly inefficient and had little idea of cargo work. Unloading continued at a slow and erratic pace, mainly due to constant air raids. There was an air raid shelter on the dockside, and when the sirens sounded, shore labor would make a mad dash for it. We, however, manned our guns at every air raid alarm and we had as many as eight to ten raids a day.

April 3rd was a particularly busy day with several air raid alarms in early and mid-morning, but no planes were spotted. Again in early afternoon, there were more alarms requiring us to man our guns each time. 1510…Air raid alarm; the Germans used four-motored bombers against the convoy for the first time. The Luftwaffe overhead was too high for machine gun action, although shore batteries were actively firing. One bomb dropped off the starboard quarter about 200 yards and one dropped off the port beam about 75 yards.

Again at 2100…Air raid alarm; the shore batteries opened fire. The *Dunboyne* and the *Eldena* opened fire on a plane passing over at about 1000 feet. The plane appeared to be hit by the fire from both ships and crashed off the starboard bow. Both the *Dunboyne* gun crew and ours opened fire on a plane which passed the barrage apparently unhit and escaped.

At the same time our aft guns fired on a plane diving on the Polish ship, *Tobruk*, on our port beam at a distance of 200 yards. The plane was hit and the pilot bailed out. A bomb had dropped in the #5 hatch of the *Tobruk*, sinking her to water level by the stern at the dock. A bomb was dropped on a building off our starboard beam 175 yards away killing several people, and three bombs fell off our port beam at 150 yards. A Junkers JU-87 Stuka dive bomber attacked the *Eldena*, strafing us with

Lecia Mae McDonald Haynes

NAVAL ARMED GUARD

COMBAT AIR CREW

NAVAL AVIATOR

LCDR John L. Haynes, USNR Retired
Naval Aviator

Armed Guard Center at Brooklyn, NY (National Archives)

Armed Guard Center at Brooklyn, NY (National Archives)

SS Eldena Sunk 8 July 1943

A convoy forming up in Iceland in World War II. (National Archives)

A seaman negotiates the slick deck of a merchant vessel coated with thick ice. If his ship were torpedoed, a sailor's chance of survival in the icy waters near the Arctic Circle was slim.

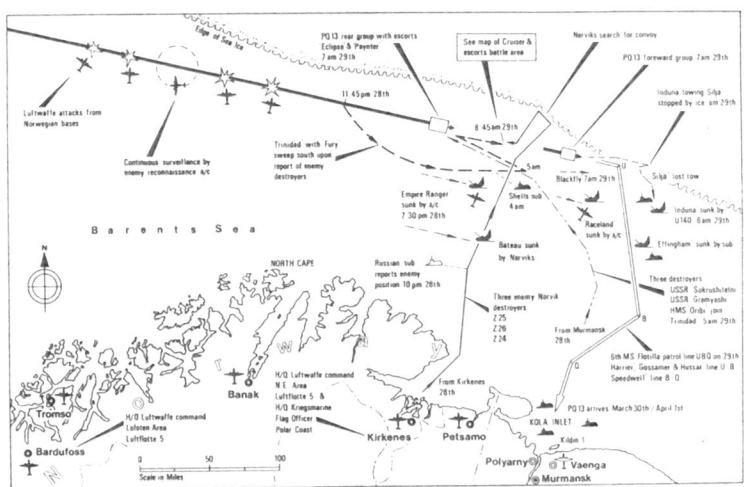

Fig: 4 Convoy P.Q.13 Battle area

BACK HOME FROM THE COLD NORTH

Seaman 1st Class John Lanier Haynes, son of Mr. and Mrs. J. I. Haynes, 2016 Starnes Street, who volunteered for the U. S. Navy Dec. 10, 1941 is now home to visit his parents on a ten day leave.

He just returned from a four months trip to Murmansk, Russia, where he and his gun crew was credited with shooting down 3 Nazi dive bombers.

It is said that the 13 is an unlucky number, but Lanier calls it his lucky number. This is why: 13th convoy to Russia, No. 13 in convoy, 13 ment in gun crew, 13 year old ship, 13 planes in cargo, docked at No. 13 pier, 13th convoy to leave Russia, 13 ships in convoy, 13 officers on ship, 13 destroyers, 13 corvets, 13 ships in convoy to leave Iceland, left on 13th of May. Add this and you have 13 13's.

A Navy photographer took official photos and sent it to the local paper in Augusta, Georgia.

ATEST PICTURE OF NAVAL HERO

This new picture of John L. Haynes, the 19-year-old Augusta seaman who was cited for gallantry in a naval letter, was made after he returned from the mission in which his exploit occurred. It is an official Navy picture. Parents of the young hero are Mr. and Mrs. John Ira Haynes. He is now at Norfolk taking trade training to become a machinist's mate.

Carrier Qualifying with the Curtis SB2C Helldiver aboard the USS Guadalcanal.

John L. Haynes, President of Alaska Society, Sons of the American Revolution at the Centennial Gala in Louisville, Kentucky, 29 April 1989. George Washington's actual signet ring, the most valued property of SAR, shown by a George Washington reenactor.

machine gun fire, but no damage was done except for holes in the mainmast crosstrees.

By 2400 when the "All Clear" sounded, we had expended 3,000 rounds of .50-caliber ammunition and 800 rounds of .30—caliber. No casualties. So ended our 4th day in the port of Murmansk.[13]

Meanwhile another saga developed at an adjoining dock. Morris Mills writes of his personal ordeal:

"At 2100hrs a bomber evading detection dived on the British freighter, *New Westminster City*, and four bombs struck, the ship igniting her into a blazing inferno. Over thirty Russians working in the holds were killed, as were several crewmembers and two Army gunners. The bomb that struck the bridge penetrated three decks before going through my cabin and exploding in the hold. The detonation of a five hundred pound bomb within feet of one's self beggars description. A column of flame blasted through the accommodation, followed by a colossal roaring sound as the cabin disintegrated. The opposite bulkhead ripped apart like tissue paper revealing, for a split second, the horrified face of the Radio Officer. I was hurled into a corner and showered with burning debris.

The conflagration of flames, the hideous sounds of metal being torn apart, mixed with the cries and screams of the wounded, drove me to a mad desperation. Frantically I tore myself free of burning wreckage and hurled myself through a jagged hole where once the door had been. Out on the open deck, I ran blindly for several yards before collapsing in an alleyway. All around me the bridge was a blazing inferno and I could feel my skin scorching. I was quite rational and knew I had to get somewhere safer, so pulled myself upright only to fall down. 'This is bloody stupid!' I thought, "What's wrong with me?" Then I saw my left foot had been smashed to a bloody pulp and was only connected to my leg by strips of sinew, the white bone protruding at the bottom. Then the waves of agony raged through me in torrents. I may have screamed in my torment. If so, it was a silent scream, for I heard nothing. I was terrified the foot was going to drop off and sat cradling the bloody object in my hands, the hot blood pumping out through my fingers."[14]

Morris O. Mills was destined to spend many months in the most primitive hospital conditions imaginable in Murmansk and Archangel, having his left foot amputated above the ankle with no morphine or any other painkillers.

William P. Short, the Scottish Engineer Officer from the torpedoed *Induna*, was another tragic casualty of the attacks. He was one of 17 survivors out of 34 who had spent four days in a lifeboat under extremely cold conditions and suffered frozen feet and legs. Both legs were amputated; one below the knee and one above. Many other survivors from bombed or torpedoed merchant ships suffered these horrendous conditions. The Russian doctors and nurses did the best they could, considering their facilities had been bombed to near extinction. The Russian war-wounded were treated the same.

Berthed immediately in front of the *New Westminster City* was the British freighter *Empire Starlight*. At about the same time, 2130 April 3rd, a wave of bombers swept in. They gave the impression of a large black shadow roaring down the quay, spitting fire. The cannon shells rippled down the quay in flashing explosions, sending lethal pieces of timber flying through the air. All around, Russians were going down like tenpins as they dived for shelter. The plane at the end of its run bombed the *Empire Starlight*, which immediately burst into flames.

Confusion reigned as the Russians attempted to deal with a multitude of tasks, fighting fires, collecting wounded and removing bodies. The wounded were half-carried and half-dragged into a nearby warehouse. Inside, the light of burning ships piercing the cracks and holes in the decrepit old wooden building broke the darkness. A group of women workers was huddled in a corner crying and wailing. As the wounded were brought in, some of the women went over and tried to comfort them, wiping blood away from their faces, and speaking soothingly as they restrained them in their agony.

April 4th...Several more air raid alarms during the morning and afternoon required us to man our guns but the only planes we saw were friendly Russians patrolling the area. At 2130 air raid alarm revealed 8 bombers overhead ready for attack. Diving on the ships at the docks and in the harbor, they dropped their deadly payload. Three bombs dropped astern of the *Eldena* within 75 to 100 yards, the concussion of which rocked the ship, but there was no damage. The next wave of bombers dropped eight bombs hitting mostly in the channel about 200 yards off the stern, and three more hit off the port beam 75 yards distant. Many of the bombs fell on parts of the town ahead about 6000 yards, starting fires. Others fell in the warehouse areas about 500 yards off our port beam, starting blazing fires. We had put up a fierce battle defending our ship, expending the remaining 1,000 rounds of .50-caliber ammunition and all but 400 rounds of .30-caliber. By 2400, "All Clear".

April 5th...0310 Air raid alarm. A single bomber overhead dropped three flares to light up the harbor, followed by a diving attack on our ship. Ensign Fink, who manned the twin .30-cal Lewis on the bridge, opened fire, expending 200 rounds of the .30-cal. ammo. Three bombs hit the dock alongside on our starboard. The bomber then circled the ship twice before being driven off by machine gun fire. The remaining 200 rounds of .30-cal. ammo were expended. We were now completely out of machine gun ammunition.[15]

Note: Convoy PQ-13 was the first convoy to feel the full fury of the German attack. Previous convoys PQ-1 through PQ-12 had all completed the Murmansk run with very little to no opposition or loss of ships. Therefore Navy suppliers had not anticipated the fury of the air attacks we would encounter, rendering our meager supply woefully inadequate.

Ensign Fink was able to receive from Ensign Brinn of the *Dunboyne* 940 rounds of .30-cal. ammo, but no .50-cal. Their ship had been issued the same amount as ours and needed their balance for their own defense.

Mr. Fink appealed to Commander Frankel, the US Naval Attaché in Murmansk, for additional ammunition. He would have to request a supply from the Russian military that had received great quantities from the arriving Allied ships. It was not until April 9th that he was able to provide 3,000 rounds of .50-caliber, of which 2,750 rounds were ball and 250 rounds were tracers.

Meanwhile on April 6, 7, and 8, daily air raids continued. Mostly we stayed aboard ship in lieu of opting for the Russian air raid shelters. From our vantage points in the gun tubs we could at least get a good view of action and we could practice "dry firing" on the incoming planes. On the 8th the shore batteries shot down one bomber. Russian planes were observed overhead frequently, patrolling the skies.

Chapter 7
ASHORE & MORE RAIDS

On April 7th, Paul Harkey and I decided to walk into town to try to buy a few souvenirs. We changed into uniform knowing the only thing the Russians respected was a uniform backed up by lots of official passes. These we presented to the gangway sentries who carefully examined them from every angle, nodding in a knowing fashion and said, "Korosho." (Good) and let us pass. We were well aware of the propensity of the Police and military to stop us and demand identity papers.

There was no local or public transportation. There were only the military trucks, tanks, or motorcycles. The local populace walked or used horse-drawn sleighs or carts. Since the whole area was covered with hard packed snow, the children scurried around on ice skates. Wandering along the rubble-strewn streets we found very few shops open and those had only cheap looking household and kitchen items...nothing we wanted to buy. There was evidence of war everywhere: bomb craters, shattered buildings, broken glass, mangled and abandoned vehicles, and pieces of shot-down German aircraft. There was one almost whole twin engine plane that appeared to have tried to land after being shot down. Nothing useful was left on the plane, and I wondered about the fate of the pilot, if he survived. The whole town was dreary and depressing. The people were suspicious of these "Capitalists" and would hardly look at us. They certainly wouldn't try to talk with us for fear of being seen by the police or KGB, and reported.

We decided to check out the Intourist Hotel and maybe get a bite to eat. Entering the lobby we found a whole new world from what we had just walked through. There were nice furnishings, much better dressed people, some higher ranking officers and a bit of English being spoken and understood. To my astonishment and delight, in the midst was a drop-dead gorgeous woman dressed in the most beautiful furs with ermine trim I had ever seen. Even her calf-length boots were of fine fur, and she walked with the poise and grace of a princess. I was in love and so was Paul. I did not find out who she was and never saw her again, but she made my day. Going to the second floor restaurant was anti-climactic but we were a bit hungry. The lunch of fish, rice, black bread and tea was not too bad, all things considered.

It was time to walk back to the ship, but before we got very far, the inevitable air-raid alarm sounded. The loud high-pitch wailing siren sent chills up the spine. We headed for an air-raid shelter nearby. It was already crowded with Russian families, workers and soldiers. We squeezed in and waited about forty-five minute before the "All Clear" sounded and we could proceed to the ship.

April 10th...One of the Armed Guard gun crew survivors from the sunken SS *Effingham*, Charles B. Covington, Jr. Seaman 2c. USN was sent aboard.

April 11th...The *Eldena* moved from her present dock over to the ammunition dock at Pier #13 and began unloading our bombs, shells, other high explosives, and drums of high-octane aviation gasoline. A direct bomb hit would completely destroy the ship, its cargo and us. Add to that the huge stockpile of munitions on the dock awaiting shipment by train to the battle front. We were all much more nervous about this new location.

Mills writes: "The bombing of Murmansk had now reached a peak of ferocity not experienced by any town in WWII. Eight to ten raids a day were not uncommon. The Germans seemed to have a set bombing pattern. First would come the Stuka dive bombers falling out of the sky with their special screaming device to terrorize the citizens. Then the JU 88's and Henkel's would over-fly, dropping 500 pound bombs. The air reverberated with engine noise, exploding bombs, and the roar of anti-aircraft guns, sending one's senses reeling to the brink of madness."[16]

April 12th...0415 Air raid alarm...only Russian planes overhead. "All Clear" at 0445. Then at 0745, another alarm. This time five Stuka dive bombers screamed down toward our ship and dock, but swerved off when they met the intense machine gun fire from our guns. Three bombs hit about 200 yards ahead of the ship. We had expended 380 rounds of .50-caliber. All clear at 0845.

April 13th...0030 Air raid alarm...German HE111 bombers overhead. Search lights scanned the skies for the planes. The shore batteries put up a barrage of AA and tracers as the bombers neared the docks. I was asleep in my bunk in the fo'c's'le and did not hear the alarm. Bombs were heard to drop in the vicinity of the docks, one of which hit less than fifty yards of the *Eldena's* port bow. The explosion and concussion severely jolted the ship, throwing me out of my bunk. Completely startled and disoriented, I groped for my coat and helmet. I had never known such fear before...the next one might be a direct hit. With a surge of adrenalin I raced to my battle station in the gun tub only to find the gun already manned. Since I had not responded to the alarm, one of the other gunners had taken over. I could only stand by, shaking like a leaf in the wind, and watch the action. I really felt useless and ashamed at missing the alarm

April 14th...Air raid alarms with firing from shore batteries but none of the bombers came within range of our guns.

A very bad day was April 15th. In the early afternoon about 50 enemy planes were in the air at one time and late in the afternoon at least 125 more planes became involved in dog fights. Two British ships were hit. Murmansk was taking a terrific pounding, but allied planes were hitting back at the attackers. Ten bombers overhead diving out of the sun dropped bombs at the head of the harbor. At 1830, twenty-five bombers were again diving out of the sun. They released their deadly bombs, eight of which hit the dock area near us and were heard as they passed overhead. Several planes drew our machine gun fire as they went past. One bomb destroyed a dock side crane, one hit an air raid shelter killing several people, and one hit the #2 hatch of the ship across the dock from us. During that afternoon's raids we expended 1400 rounds of .50-caliber ammo.

April 16th…Not nearly so many air raid alarms on this day. We had finished unloading at Pier #13, the ammunition dock, and at 1400 we moved out into the harbor and anchored.

April 17th, 18th & 20th…At anchor in the harbor; we were no longer primary targets for the bombers. We could see lots of action over the town and docks and hear the explosions and AA fire from the shore batteries, but we were not threatened.

April 19th…Convoy PQ-14 arrived. It had started out with twenty-seven vessels, thirteen of which were British, ten USA flag, two Russian, one Dutch and one Panamanian. The convoy with Commodore Captain Rees RNR, on board the British *S.S. Empire Howard*, sailed from Reykjavik on the afternoon of the April 8th. After 30 hours of fog, and 12 hours in heavy Polar ice only eight ships remained in company, the rest having returned to Iceland with ice damage. The convoy entered the port of Murmansk, with its escort increased by two Russian destroyers and with fighter planes overhead. Only two ships in the convoy had Armed Guards aboard; the SS *Yaka* and the SS *West Cheswald*. While in port the ships shared in the daily attacks which PQ-13 was receiving. The *West Cheswald* was lucky enough to escape damage from enemy action while at Murmansk. On the morning of April 23rd a bomb fell fifty feet from the *Yaka* that damaged the ship and destroyed a 50 ton crane which had been used in unloading tanks from the ship. The *Yaka* had a long stay in Murmansk because she required repairs to her bow and propeller, and missed sailing with the convoy which left on April 28.[17]

April 21st…The *Eldena* moved to the water dock to take on provisions for the return voyage to Iceland and the United States. Our CO, Ensign Fink, chose this time to visit Naval Attaché, Commander Frankel, to get a resupply of machine gun ammunition. We had almost depleted the 3000 rounds he had provided for us earlier. Commander Frankel assured Mr. Fink he would do his best. In the meantime on the 22nd *Eldena* moved from the water dock back out to anchor in the harbor. It took several days and Commander Frankel had to beg the Russians for the munitions we needed, reminding them that it was *Eldena* and *Dunboyne* who had put up the best fight of all the ships and shot down six of the bombers. They acknowledged the kills and provided both ships with the needed munitions which now had to be delivered by small boat to the ships at anchor.

April 23rd thru 26th the *Eldena* and other ships that had off-loaded their cargo, lay at anchor in the harbor awaiting the formation of a return convoy. Every day and at all hours German planes bombed and strafed the town and docks. They paid very little attention to the empty ships in the harbor. The shore batteries and the Russian Air Force valiantly defended the area, shooting down a number of German planes.

April 27th....A small boat came alongside, delivering our much needed munitions. We were very grateful Commander Frankel had come through for us. Also on the small boat were survivors of the *Effingham* who would sail home with us.

Seaman 2c, Charles B. Covington, USN, 17 of Halifax Co. Virginia, had already boarded on April 10th.

The others were merchant seamen:

Lewis S, Hathaway, 25, of Middleboro, Mass.
Maynard R. Richardson, 35, of Allston, Mass.
J. Easterling, 30, of Higdon, Georgia
Charles A. Hunnefield, 22, of Boston Mass.
Clifford A. Jensen, 23, of Chicago, Ill.

Chapter 8
CONVOY QP-11 LEAVES MURMANDSK

April 28, 1942...Convoy QP-11 got underway to sea with thirteen merchant ships:

British ships to the UK were: *Briarwood, Dan-Y-Bryn, Trehata,* and *Atheltemplar.*

Russian ship to the UK: *Tsiolkovsky*

Panamanian ships to the USA: *Stone Street, El Estero, Gallant Fox* and *Ballot.*

American ships to the USA: *Dunboyne, Eldena, Mormacmar,* and *West Cheswald.*

Escorts were eight British destroyers, six corvettes, and one trawler, also two Russian destroyers and five minesweepers. The convoy Commodore was the captain of *Briarwood,* Vice Commodore the captain of *Dan-Y-Bryn.*

April 29th...The British cruiser HMS *Edinburgh,* which had been in Murmansk loading a five ton quantity of gold bullion (payment by the Russians to the U.S. and U.K. for war supplies delivered) joined the convoy but then moved out, taking station ahead of the convoy. Several destroyers and corvettes also moved ahead, leaving four destroyers and three corvettes. The *Edinburgh's* presence was reported by German reconnaissance planes and U-boats.

April 30th...The *Edinburgh,* commanded by Rear-Admiral Sir Stuart Bonham-Carter also had aboard some thirty injured survivors for repatriation to the UK. He had visited with each of them, and before leaving made a short speech. "Well, lads, you know we are escorting

JOHN L. HAYNES

Convoy QP-11 back to England. I don't think our German friends are going to let us pass without a fight, so you must prepare yourselves for action, but never fear, you are in the hands of the Royal Navy and we'll get you back safely." Stirring words.[18]

That afternoon the *Edinburgh* was hit while zig-zagging ahead of the convoy by two torpedoes fired by U-456. Her stern was blown off, and she started back towards Murmansk, 250 miles away, at slow speed, escorted by two destroyers. The U-boat meanwhile shadowed the lame cruiser, and the weakening of the convoy escort encouraged the enemy to send three destroyers to sea that night.[19]

May 1st...My 19th birthday. I wondered how we would celebrate the momentous occasion!! It didn't take long to find out...At 0445 six Junker JU88 torpedo planes attacked. Four of them came directly at us while two climbed into the clouds. Of the four on attack, two flew across our stern toward the ship aft of us, but turned off when both our ships opened fire. Both planes were observed to drop a torpedo but no tracks were seen. The other two bombers flew toward the ship ahead of us but veered off when we opened fire. Both, however, were seen to release their torpedoes. None of the torpedoes hit their intended targets. A plane flew around the convoy but was kept at a distance by gunfire from the escort ships. Our approximate position was 25°40' E/74°10'N. We had expended about 230 rounds of .50-caliber ammo.

1245 "Flags" got the visual signal "Jig How" from the escorts of impending surface raider attack by German destroyers. They made no less than five separate attempts to reach the convoy, but were each time foiled by the aggressive tactics of the far weaker British escort, which was most ably led by Commander M. Richmond in the aptly-named *Bulldog*. One of our small force, the *Amazon*, was damaged, and one Russian merchant ship, *Tsiolkovsky*, which had straggled, was sunk by an enemy destroyer's torpedo. I was watching as the torpedo struck and saw the ship sink, stern first, in only a few seconds. Only five of the Russian crew survived to be picked up by the rescue ship.

Throughout the afternoon, from 1400 till nearly 1800, the enemy's repeated lunges at the convoy were successfully driven off. Finally, the Germans abandoned the attempt and went off to find the damaged

Edinburgh. To Commander Richmond's congratulatory signal to his consorts one of them instantly replied, "I should hate to play poker with you", and there is indeed no doubt that he thoroughly outfought the enemy's 'three of a kind'.[20]

1600…The convoy encountered heavy floe ice and icebergs requiring formation in single column to get through. The ice thinned and began to separate somewhat, and after getting through, the ships reformed to the original convoy order.

Meanwhile the HMS *Edinburgh*, unable to steer except with her engines, and also unable to be towed, was making very slow progress eastwards. On the evening of May 1st she was joined by four minesweepers, but early the following morning the German destroyers found her. A series of confused fights followed, and the cruiser herself, for all her disablement and grievous trouble, managed to hit and stop the large destroyer *Hermann Schoemann*.

But the *Forester* was also heavily hit, just at the moment when the enemy had fired torpedoes. By ill luck one of these, almost at the end of its run, hit the *Edinburgh* amidships on the opposite side to her earlier damage. She was unable to take any avoiding action. The ship was thus almost cut in two. She continued to fight her armament, and one enemy described her gunfire even then as being "extraordinarily good", but she was plainly doomed.

Another misfortune followed quickly, when the *Foresight*, the last effective destroyer, was badly hit and brought to a standstill. There were thus three British ships all lying stopped at the same time, and all with much of their armament out of action. The two surviving enemies could have finished them off at leisure, but chose instead to take off the crew of the damaged *Schoemann*. This they successfully accomplished. The *Schoemann* sank and the other German destroyers then withdrew.

The *Forester* and *Foresight* next managed to get under way at slow speed, the minesweepers took off the *Edinburgh's* crew, among whom casualties were remarkably light, and the cruiser was then sunk by one of our own torpedoes. The enemy had undoubtedly scored a success; but he might have annihilated our whole force had he not mistaken the minesweepers for destroyers and, we now know, greatly overestimated the opposition by which he was faced.[21]

Note: HMS Edinburgh was known to have been carrying gold on her last voyage. The gold was part of Russia's war payments to the U.S and the U.K. for materials delivered. Most of that gold was recovered. In April 1981, the survey ship Dammtor began searching for the wreck in the Barents Sea. After only ten days, they discovered the ship's final resting place at an approximate position of 72°N 35°W 72°N 35°W, at a depth of 245 meters (800 ft). It was not until 15 September 1981 when a diver finally penetrated the bomb room and recovered a bar of gold. On 7 October, bad weather finally forced the suspension of diving operations, but by that time, 431 of 465 ingots had been recovered, now worth in excess of £43,000,000 sterling.[22]

May 2nd...0815. One unidentified plane, believed to be long range enemy reconnaissance, circled the convoy at a distance no doubt reporting our position and status.

0945...The east-bound convoy PQ-15 had entered the critical part of its passage. It was powerfully escorted, and covered by Admiral Tovey's full strength. Up to the 2nd of May no losses had been suffered. On this day the west-bound convoy (QP-11) was passed, and a gloomy prognostication of what probably lay ahead was received from its escort.[23]

1015...Our escorts detected submarine activity in the area and the corvettes and destroyers dropped depth charges on the starboard bow of the convoy. 1400...Again the escorts were dropping depth charges, this time astern of the convoy. We were also being shadowed by circling enemy reconnaissance planes.

May 3rd...Two British cruisers believed to be of the *Southampton* type were observed on the horizon steaming parallel to the convoy. The cruisers sent out two scout planes to circle the convoy for possible enemy activity.

May 4th...Two escort destroyers left the convoy, later returned then left again. Meanwhile floating mines were sighted on two separate occasions.

May 5th & 6th...Friendly planes circled the convoy.

May 7th...We anchored in the harbor at Reykjavik, Iceland.

Chapter 9
HOMEWARD BOUND

"These Russian convoys are becoming a regular millstone around our necks, and cause a steady attrition in both cruisers and destroyers."

Admiral Pound (First Sea Lord) to Fleet Admiral King, U.S.N. (Chief of Naval Operations), 18th May, 1942[24]

On November 2, 1945, Admiral King wrote: "*During the past three and a half years, the Navy has been dependent upon the Merchant Marine to supply our far-flung fleet and bases. Without this support, the Navy could not have accomplished its mission. Consequently, it is fitting that the Merchant Marine share in our success as it shared in our trials.*"[25]

Merchant ships lost in convoys PQ-13, QP-11 or in port in Murmansk during the period March 20 to May 7, 1942:

American: *SS Ballot, SS Raceland, SS Bateau, SS Effingham, SS Harpalion,*

British: *Empire Cowper, Induna, Empire Starlight, Empire Ranger, New Westminster City*

Polish: *Tobruk*

Russian: *Tsiolkovsky*

May 9th…A broken spider or crowsfoot from the aft 4"/50 gun was taken ashore to the Port Directors Office in Reykjavik to be welded and returned in two days. Crews maintained anchor watches.

May 12th…Crowsfoot was not returned to the Port Directors Office as hoped for. The ships machinist made a substitute to be used until one could be obtained. Even though we were in the harbor for six days, none of the crew was allowed ashore.

May 13th 0500...Underway to sea, bound for Halifax, Nova Scotia. The convoy consisted of thirteen merchant ships, one U.S. destroyer and one U.S. Coast Guard cutter. The twin Lewis guns mounted atop the wheel house had to be removed as they were causing magnetic interference with the compass. The ammunition was moved to the after-deck house. At 1730 the cutter dropped depth charges on the starboard quarter of the convoy. Again at 2045 the cutter dropped depth chargers on the starboard quarter.

May 16th...1300...Our convoy joined another of twenty-nine ships, two British destroyers and four British corvettes. The total merchant ships were now forty-six with six escorts. Soon the U.S. Coast Guard cutter and destroyer left the convoy.

May 18th...1620...One of the corvettes signaled that a submarine was detected on the port bow and dropped two depth charges. Two corvettes and one destroyer searched the area for about one hour. Nothing further. 2150...A signal from a merchant ship reported a submarine sighted on the port beam. The crew manned the surface gun but it turned out to be a whale.

May 19th...2030. Three depth charges dropped by corvettes on the port beam. Two corvettes and one destroyer searched the area; nothing further.

May 20th...0030...Airplane passed directly overhead believed to be a twin engine Airliner bound for Iceland...0700. Friendly plane circled the convoy. 1200. Signal from the Commodore to keep a sharp lookout for submarines from today.

May 22nd...1430...Two British destroyers and one corvette joined the convoy.

May 25th...1530...We anchored in Bedford Basin, Halifax, Nova Scotia. We had sailed a distance of 2364 miles at an average speed of 7.93 knots.

This last leg of the voyage had been quite pleasant. There had been no real threat from the enemy, the seas were moderate to almost calm, the temperature had been really warm compared to what we had been through, and the thought of going home to the U.S.A. kept us elated. I couldn't wait to set foot on American soil and to be able to call my folks back in Georgia.

May 27th...1400. A convoy of ten merchant ships departed Halifax for New York City. Just outside the harbor we were joined by a convoy of thirty-two ships, also west bound, escorted by two British corvettes and one destroyer.

May 28th...U.S. Navy patrol planes were seen frequently.

May 29th...The convoy dispersed and the *Eldena* entered the Cape Cod Canal.

May 30th...The SS *Eldena* docked at Pier #2, Staten Island, New York, and Ensign Fink reported to the Port Director. "WE ARE HOME!!!" It was hard to believe we were finally home. We were ecstatic.

In his report to the Chief of Naval Operations, Washington, D.C., Ensign Fred S. Fink, USNR, Commanding Officer of Armed Guard Detail, SS *Eldena*, recommended the following:

All machine guns be supplied with shrapnel shields over the barrels of the guns and colored sun visors for the gunners. Also that the Lewis machine guns be supplied with large size (97) round pans.

The caliber of anti-aircraft battery is insufficient. It is recommended that all ships entering aircraft operation zones be supplied with anti-aircraft guns of caliber of 20 millimeter or larger, plus sufficient amount of ammunition to successfully repel aircraft attacks. This ship was without ammunition after the second air raid and only through the Naval Attaché, Commander Frankel, were we able to procure more ammunition.

The issued cold weather clothing (submarine gear) was not adequate. Recommend the following be issued in addition to the submarine gear:

Heavy woolen underwear
Felt or sheepskin lined boots
Sheepskin lined hats with ear tabs
Knee length sheepskin lined canvas coats with hoods
Heavy sheepskin lined waterproof mittens

Proper clothing is extremely necessary for required efficiency in cold weather and would suggest the British winter kit for the Arctic Ocean as a model for proper clothing.[26]

Departing the SS *Eldena* was kind of sad; she had been our duty station and home for more than four months, and we had grown quite fond of the old "Rust Bucket". We would also miss the seamen of the Merchant Marine. We had lived and worked together during many life-threatening attacks by German aircraft, submarines and surface raiders. They had helped in every way they could during the ferocious onslaught of the enemy. Gone was the initial minor friction and jibes between us at the beginning of the voyage.

We would also miss our Commanding Officer, Ensign Fred Fink. He was a very good leader who treated us fairly, firmly, and respectfully, and that respect was returned. As for the Gun Crew itself, very few would be together on our next assigned ship. The policy was to assign experienced gunners to newly formed crews to help the "green-horns" learn the ropes.

All of the enlisted men of the crew reported to the Armed Guard Center in Brooklyn, there to blend in with the thousands living there awaiting further assignment. First we were debriefed by Intelligence Officers who wanted to learn as much as possible about the enemy attacks and the Russian port of Murmansk. I was asked if I had kept a diary. I had kept a small one. He asked to see it and said he'd have to keep it for a while and would return it later. I never saw it again. We then got thorough physical examinations, collected our mail and back pay, then were issued new uniforms and allowed to go on liberty for the first time. We also got promoted. I was now a Seaman First Class.

On my first liberty I felt kind of strange. I didn't want to go anywhere particularly. I just wanted to walk around freely without fear of air raids, bombs falling, or Russian police watching my every move. I did a bit of window shopping, marveling at the supply of items available as opposed to the meager, dreary Murmansk shops. I wandered into a drugstore and sat at the soda fountain.

"What'll-ya-have, Sailor?" said the clerk, speaking "Brooklynese." "I think I'll have a big bowl of ice cream", I said. "Lemme fix ya up", he said.

So he got a large honeydew melon, cut it in half and filled the cavity with the best vanilla ice cream I had ever tasted. I ate the ice cream, bowl and all. Man what a treat!! "How much do I owe you?" "Not a thing…On the house…Welcome home, Sailor", he said. Man it was good to be home! What a great country! I wandered around for while longer, then walked back to the Center and hit the sack for some much needed quiet rest.

Chapter 10
STATESIDE DUTY

A ten day leave at home, in Augusta, Georgia, where it was warm and safe, was a welcome relief. Being the first of the Augusta volunteers to return from an active war zone sparked the interest of the media and of several people who wanted to learn about the action first hand. A prominent lawyer, Isaac Peebles, asked me to visit with him and tell him of my experiences. During the meeting he asked if I was where I wanted to be in the Navy. I confessed that my real goal was in aviation and that I hoped, someday, to be a pilot. Nothing more was said about that, and I soon returned to the Armed Guard Center in Brooklyn to await my next assignment.

In the meantime, on June 8th, the Center received a call from Admiral Fairfield informing them that Armed Guard crew of the SS *Eldena* had shot down three German bombers in the harbor of Murmansk. The Russian Government had rewarded the entire crew of the vessel with one month's pay.

After about a fortnight in Brooklyn a summons "John L. Haynes, Seaman 1st Class, report to the Officer of the Day" sounded over the loud speaker. What had I done? Why was I being called before the O.D.? "Haynes, why are you using P.I. to get out of the Armed Guard?" "I'm sorry, Sir, I don't know what P.I. is, and I am not trying to get out of the Armed Guard." The Officer of the Day said, "P.I. is Political Influence, and we have a letter from the Navy Department stating that Congressman Carl Vincent of Georgia desires that you be offered your choice of an appointment to the Naval Academy, an assignment to the Naval Aviation

Cadets, or to the Aviation Mechanics School. What is your choice?" In a state of shock, I was unable to make a choice. "May I give you my answer tomorrow, Sir?" "You may. Dismissed."

What a decision to make! Having been only an average student in high school and having no college whatever, the thought of going to the Naval Academy or to Aviation Cadets and risking failure was a great concern. Besides, I still had my heart set on becoming one of the prestigious enlisted pilots in the Naval Aviation Pilots (NAP) program. I reasoned that I could do well as an aircraft mechanic and could later apply for the N.A.P. Satisfied with that decision, I applied for Aviation Mechanics School and soon after was ordered to the Naval Air Station at Norfolk, Virginia, to begin my training.

I was assigned to Class 25, Section 4, which was made up of raw recruits fresh out of boot camp, Apprentice Seamen who had succeeded in being assigned to this special aviation school. They noticed that I was a Seaman 1c and was wearing a campaign ribbon of the European Theater of Operations, and asked questions about my past duty. When I tried to tell them a bit about it, they didn't believe me and scoffed, saying, "You're full of bull." So I just clammed up and said nothing more.

After learning that attorney Isaac Peebles had written to or contacted Georgia Congressman Carl Vincent on my behalf to get this great new assignment, I wrote him a letter thanking him for his help. It is doubtful that I could have achieved this goal without his intervention. It not only changed my life in the Navy but also helped to prepare me for my later career. The following letter was his response:

ISAAC S. PEEBLES, JR
ATTORNEY AT LAW
MARION BUILDING
AUGUSTA, GA.

July 10, 1942

Mr. J. L. Haynes, Sea. 1 C,
Class 25, Sec. 4,
A. M. M. School, N.A.S.,
Norfolk, VA.

Dear Mr. Haynes:

I have always maintained that a go-getter will get there in the end. You have about you that indefinable something which means ultimate success. It was because of this that you sold yourself to me. I trust that I contributed some small mite toward your transfer. If so, I am most gratified.

I bespeak for you a most successful career. There is no reason why you should not succeed in any undertaking. You have a good father and a good mother who have been willing to make any sort of sacrifices for you. You have shown that you deserve their sacrifices, and I am sure that the future will demonstrate that you are worthy of them all.

May God bless you and keep you is the prayer of a sinner.

Sincerely yours,
Isaac S. Peebles, Jr.
ISAAC S. PEEBLES, JR.

ISP:LM

September 1942, the entire Naval Air Station was in full Dress Blues for inspection and parade. The top ranking officers were on a platform draped with colors, the United States flag and the Navy flag were displayed, the band was playing, and all was in readiness. The band stopped playing, and an officer stepped to the microphone, "John L. Haynes, Seaman First Class, front and center." From far back in the ranks where the Training School students stood at attention, I almost fainted! Recovering, I marched to the platform where Admiral Buckner, the Commanding Officer, returned my salute. The Admiral read the following letter:

* * *

SEP 5 1942
From: The Chief of Naval Personnel.
To: HAYNES, John Lanier, Sea1c, USN.

Via: The Commanding Officer, U. S. Naval Air Station,
Naval Operating Base, Norfolk' Va.

Subject: Commendation

The Chief of Naval Personnel takes pleasure in commending you for your conduct as a member of the Armed Guard crew of merchant vessel, SS Eldena, which had numerous encounters with enemy airplanes, submarines, and surface vessels, and for shooting down three enemy bombers.

Your conduct on the occasions referred to is in keeping with the highest traditions of the Naval Service.

A copy of this letter has been made a part of your official records in the Bureau.

L. E. Denfold
The Assistant Chief of Naval Personnel

* * *

This was our last inspection at NOB Norfolk. My classmates no longer scoffed, but now accepted me as an "Old Salt".

Chapter 11
FLYING HIGH

The Aviation Training Center was relocated to the small town of Millington, Tennessee, some twenty miles outside of Memphis, and called the Memphis Naval Air Training Facility. At this location, our training continued on through the fall where completing all courses with top grades, I was promoted to Aviation Machinists Mate, Petty Officer Third Class, or as the Navy rates it, AMM3c.

January 1943, after another short home leave, I reported as ordered to the Naval Air Station, Floyd Bennett Field, Brooklyn, New York. Assigned to a squadron of fighter aircraft and torpedo bombers, VC-24 or Composite Squadron #24, I was appointed as Plane Captain of a beautiful big new Grumman TBF torpedo bomber. I loved the airplane and kept it sparkling clean and in perfect condition. I still wanted to fly and took every opportunity for a flight. When the Squadron Commander asked for volunteers for turret gunners in the TBF, I immediately stepped forward. Being the only Petty Officer to have any previous gunnery training or experience, I was appointed Petty Officer in charge of the Combat Air Crews. Now I was flying on a regular basis—not as a pilot, but I was flying.

The next three months were filled with intensive operational practice of torpedo runs and gunnery. Several flights a day and at night low level runs simulating torpedo attacks were made on "enemy targets", some as single airplanes and some in step-down three plane formation. It was the latter that almost proved fatal.

On February 25th 1943, we were in a three plane step-down formation flying very low over rough seas off Long Island. The crew was Ensign Manker as pilot, Edwards as radioman, and Haynes as turret gunner. We were flying left wing position when the propeller hit the crest of a high wave. The heavy jolt of the propeller strike was followed instantly by another thud as the tail also hit the wave. The TBF was flying again, but in serious trouble. The vibration of the damaged prop took its toll and the engine caught fire and began to smoke heavily. Realizing we were going to have to ditch, we braced ourselves as best we could. Moments later the first impact was felt, then two skips on waves and headlong into another, flipping over as the plane came to rest. Now with the plane upside down and filling rapidly with icy water, getting out before she sank became paramount. I released the latch on the turret escape hatch and tried to push it outward, but the water pressure was too great at first. More water filled the turret, and then another heave and the escape hatch slid open.

My memory is blank on the actual escape. Then I was at the surface about the same time as Ens. Manker. We had emerged on the same side of the plane but had crossed under the wing somehow. I came up at the leading edge and he came up at the trailing edge, but where was Edwards? He was nowhere to be seen and the TBF was sinking, engine first. The torpedo bay doors were open and we saw him through the glass window as the aft compartment was filling with water. Breaking the glass we were able to pull him through the window to safety. We were all alive and floating.

The next few minutes were critical to survival. I believe that by Divine providence a fishing boat was nearby and dragged three wet, freezing, airmen aboard. They cut off our wet clothes and wrapped us in sacks by the coal heater in the bow of the boat. Hours later we were taken to a Coast Guard station and put to bed, covered with heated blankets and given hot soup. I was never so cold in my life, not even in the Arctic Ocean. Long Island Sound was frozen over and the ocean water offshore must have been near freezing. In a few days we were back in full operation. Flying at low levels, however, still made me uneasy for the next week or so.

JOHN L. HAYNES

Still wanting to pilot the airplane myself rather than being a gunner, I began in earnest to try to get flight training. I learned that the "NAP" program had a long waiting list and it might be years before I could be accepted. An Aviation Cadet Program called "V-5" was now offered to enlisted men who could meet the requirements. In March of 1943 I made a request for the program. The written exams and the strict physical tests were completed successfully. Now the agony of waiting for a slot in the program began.

VC-24 was fast becoming combat ready and we were assigned regular crews. My pilot was Lieutenant James H. Smith, a former Pan American "Clipper" Captain. He was older (age 34) than most of the other pilots, far more experienced, and the best pilot in the squadron as far as I was concerned. I was honored to be in his crew. Our radioman was named Christenot. Chris had also requested and successfully completed the flight training tests, so we were both waiting for a slot. We felt ours was the best team in the squadron. By this time it was mid-June and I had been promoted to AMM2c.

Note: In December 1927, James H. Smith had learned how to fly a Curtiss JN-4 "Jenny" under instructions of Charles Lindbergh, who had recently returned from his transatlantic flight. Smith enlisted in the U. S. Navy and was a naval aviator from 1933 to 1941. He returned to active service in 1943, and served in the Navy for another ten years, retiring in 1953, having attained the rank of Captain. Lt. Smith was engaged in several air battles in the Pacific, promoted and assigned to the Admiral's Staff. In 1953, President Dwight D. Eisenhower named Smith Assistant Secretary of the Navy (AIR) and Smith held this office from July 23, 1953 until June 20, 1956.

In May 1943, VC-24 was assigned to the USS *Belleau Wood*. She was a beautiful new light aircraft carrier, designated CVL-24, built on a cruiser hull and was very sleek and fast.

After the pilots completed their qualifying landings aboard the carrier, we departed on a shakedown cruise in the Caribbean. Most of the exercises were conducted near the Island of Trinidad and the Gulf of Paria, just off the coast of South America.

"Chris" and I learned that our orders to the V-5 Aviation Cadet program had been received and we were to report to Boston within three weeks for more physical exams and further processing. Panic and anxiety!! We were thousands of miles away from Boston and unsure when the carrier would be in port state-side, where we could depart. Lt. Smith requested permission to fly us to Miami where we could catch a train and report by the deadline of 0800, July 5th, 1943. The Captain refused. We would have to wait until the carrier returned to Norfolk.

The next two and one half weeks were the longest of my lifetime. The carrier docked in Norfolk July 4th and Chris and I were the first down the gangway, running for a taxi to the train depot. Riding all night, we arrived at the Boston Naval Base at 0755, July 5th.

Having passed the initial hurdles, we received orders to the Flight Preparatory School, Wesleyan University, Middleton, Connecticut, for ground school and extensive physical training. Three months can do a lot to toughen-up a scrawny kid like me. It was hard work but enjoyable.

The first actual flying was done at VPI in Blacksburg, Virginia, under the War Training School program, a civilian contract school where the flight instructors were also civilians. The flying was the equivalent of a Private Pilot's course, flown in Piper Cubs and Navy N3N's. My first solo flight was on Oct. 20th, after 6.6 hours of dual instructions.

I wrote Mom: *"After the instructor got out of the Cub, it was so light that it climbed like a homesick angel."*

Solo…That is probably the most exciting time of a fledgling pilot's life. After some 38 hours in the Cub we stepped up to the Navy N3N for twelve hours in the bi-wing open cockpit airplane. Now that's *flying!* 50 hours of flying time so far!

Pre-flight training at the University of North Carolina, Chapel Hill, occupied the next three months. No flying, just ground school and physical training. The family visited me at Christmas. My two beautiful sisters caused quite a stir among the cadets. Many wanted to talk with them and give them their addresses, hoping to get letters or "care packages".

Primary Flight School was conducted at Naval Air Station, Bunker Hill, Indiana. My instructor was Ensign John Clevenger. It was then the spring of 1944 and still cold in the flat lands of Indiana. After 9 hours in the famous old trainer, the N2S "Yellow Peril" another open cockpit bi-wing plane, I was flying solo again. No one can explain the thrill of these flights, they must be experienced. More advanced flying included aerobatics, close-formation flying, small field landings on round mats, and night flying. It was mid-June and some 100 flight hours later when this phase was completed.

During this period the Navy had determined that they had more than enough pilot trainees in the pipeline and started a purge to weed out all but the top achievers. During the week of May 8th, 14 cadets were washed out and sent to Great Lakes Boot Camp. The following week 51 more cadets were washed out and sent to Boot Camp. I felt very blessed to have survived, and worked hard to stay in the program. I was able to stay in the upper ten percent of my class all the way through the training.

Naval Air Station, Pensacola, Florida, was the site of the final part of the training programs. There we flew the Vultee SNV, and the North American SNJ. Instrument flying, navigation over land and water, combat fighter tactics, bombing, gunnery, close-formation and field carrier landings were practiced. It was during this time that Ted Williams, the famous baseball player, was one of my instructors. Just prior to completing the training, we were checked out in a real war plane, the Douglas SBD "Dauntless" Dive Bomber, and flew it about 12 hours.

February 20, 1945, was Graduation Day. My parents and two sisters came down from Augusta, Georgia, for the occasion. At the ceremony I received my Commission as an Ensign in the U.S. Naval Reserve, and awarded my Gold Wings as a Naval Aviator. I had the pleasure of having my mother pin on my Gold Wings and my sisters each pinned on a Gold Ensign bar. This was one of the proudest days of my life. I had achieved the goal I had set for myself when I joined the Navy.

I had two weeks home leave and then went to operational training at Naval Air Station, Jacksonville, Florida, where we formed a Dive Bomber Squadron, flying the Curtis SB2C, "Helldiver". This was a single pilot aircraft. There was no dual instruction. You got familiar with the plane and got in and flew it. Flying now became much more serious.

Pilots in war planes were preparing for war. There were long over-water navigation flights, dive bombing, gunnery, fighter tactics, field carrier landing practice, and finally the actual Carrier Qualification aboard the jeep carrier USS *Guadalcanal*. It was by then August 1945.

The Squadron, officially named VB-97, was relocated to NAS, Grosse Ile, Michigan for continued operational readiness and to await assignment to carrier duty in the Pacific Theater. Active combat duty for VB-97 was not to be. The Japanese surrendered to Allied Forces on September 2, 1945. The war was over.

Released from active duty October 25, 1945, I returned home to Augusta, Georgia, to begin life as a civilian. Flight instructing for a civilian flight school and duty in the Naval Air Reserve units kept me active in flying. Through the years that followed, I flew a wide variety of Naval aircraft, such as: F4U-4 Corsair, Martin AM-1, PBY-5A Catalina Flying Boat, P2V Neptune, Douglas R4D-8 (Super DC-3) and the Douglas R5D (DC-4). Staying active in the Naval Air Reserve provided responsibility and opportunity for promotion. By 1956 the permanent commission of Lieutenant Commander in the United States Naval Reserve was issued, and in July 1965, I elected to transfer to Retired Reserve status.

Note: *One the largest, most modern, hi-tech Aircraft Carrier in the United States Navy today, is the* **USS Carl Vincent**. *This mighty vessel of modern war-fare is named for the* **Honorable Carl Vincent**, *United States Representative from Georgia who served from 1914 to 1965. . During his tenure in the U.S. House, Vinson was a champion for national defense and especially the U.S. Navy and the U.S. Marine Corps This is the same Congressman Carl Vincent who helped me to get into Naval Aviation. I am forever grateful to him and Attorney Isaac Peebles for their help.*

Appendix I

THE MURMANSK RUN BY S.C. MYERS
Nov. 21, 2009
By permission of Steve Myers

I'll spin you a story of heartbreak—and glory—
Of disaster and triumph, and loss;
To a port we remember, in June—or November,
Where scarce a day lives without frost.

Murmansk is a city, hand-hewn, without pity,
A big-muscled, town, never nice!
But, at sixty-nine North, its primary worth
Was warm currents that spared it from ice.

As for winter—dear Lord, do not utter the word!
As a monster sea crashes and rails,
Ship hulls freeze and grumble; believers grow humble,
And the faithless few quake at the gales!

It's a long, lonely journey not attempted by many,
That's finished by fewer than start,
For, the might of the Main joined a Teutonic bane,
And conspired to tear us apart.

We were fated to sally down a murderous alley
Not knowing the sea or its lay.
Only nautical rangers might master the dangers
Confronting us, each passing day.

JOHN L. HAYNES

It was almost a joke, when our convoy raised smoke
To witness the faltering pace,
Where the speed of advance, like a languorous dance,
Played out as a crawl—not a race!

Our escorts were few. If the tars ever knew
Though the dashing four-stackers were brave—
They were worn out—too old—for harsh work in the cold,
On a path to a watery grave.

A gantlet in gray, with no rest on the way In the summer, bright day shone for aye!
Then and ill-wind was meant as Germania sent
Every bomb-laden crate that could fly!
In winter, withal, and the mountain-waves tall,

Even Hitler's appointed stood down,
But some U-boats surveilled as the arctic winds wailed,
And pounced on the stragglers they found.
Incessant and grim, an unwanted swim

Faced the sailors, who'd vainly attempt
With bullets and cries—to claw from the skies,
The attackers Herr Goering had sent.
In the fullness of time, despite reason or rhyme,

The attackers drew back and went home.
But the damages done 'neath a wan winter sun
Left many a brave ship—a tomb.
Then, war held its breath, and drew back its wrath,

In time for the Russians to come
As the sickle-flags wavy, announced the Red Navy
Would shield us to Murmansk—its home.
And so, battered and burned, old lessons re-learned,

FROZEN FURY

We stood into tall Kil'din's roads.
There we'd wait for a while, 'til our rank or our file
Received orders to dock and unload.

The Russians, though weary of war were not teary!
They shrugged off the bombing and fire,
Received guns and tanks with grim, hopeful thanks,
And a courage one had to admire.

Just to see, one could tell they were going through hell
At the hands of a devilish foe,
But the natives slogged on, determined to win,
And forgot their political woe.

In this way the weeks passed, until one day, at last,
We emptied of cargo—and then
We loaded anew, as merchantmen do,
Making ready for sea, once again.

During weeks that ensued, the ongoing feud
Between Nazis and Allies went on.
As Dorniers and Henkels bombs liberally sprinkled,
Our gunners earned fame, every one.

Now patched and refueled—restowed and retooled,
A convoy took shape, as before,
And in wide Kola Bay ships prepared to make way
Down an ice road to hell, in the war.

Hitler would wait, with his hordes and his hate,
But surely would test us anew;
Then, one morning in May, we got underway;
After hoisting the Red, White, and Blue.

JOHN L. HAYNES

Assigned ample pluck, from our mast to the truck,
With weary prows greeting the foam;
And that flag, smartly waving, unscathed and uncraven,
We hoisted the 'hook' and went home.

Oh, the Germans were there—had made ready with care,
To greet, as we slowly returned,
"Who cares?" one man cried, as the freighter beside
Took two 'eels' and then sank as she burned.

That continuous fight lasted seven long nights,
With six hellish days in between,
"Who cares?" once again seemed a fair question, when
The worst days were yet to be seen.

Jerry found and rejoined, precious safety purloined,
For he hunted this time as a team;
Seven U-boats encountered: nine merchantmen foundered
Survival became a bad dream.

Another long week showed the prospects were bleak
The ships would get through it unscathed.
"Unscathed?" said the Bosun, "Take a look at the ocean!
"We'll be fortunate just to be saved!"

Then, a clear morning dawned and the German's were gone;
On a day when there was no alarm,
Grim Iceland slipped by and a blue western sky
Seemed to hint at diminishing harm.

A sailor, delighted, gave a yell when he sighted
A gray dot approaching and slow;
Then, we all caught a glimpse of the two Navy blimps—
As we slogged along, slowly, below.

FROZEN FURY

Referred to as: "Mother," the gray bags gave cover,
And the U-boats knew well of their sting,
Fritz' head was down while they loitered around
On a leisurely flight and without wings.

What one might expect, and hear or see next
Was a long-legged "Dumbo" from shore,
That welcome redeemer—a slow Catalina,
Bolstered hope in the weary of war.

It remained that the fight now continued at night,
When the gray wolves were safe from the sun,
In truth, it was hasty to assume now that safety
Would take us to where we'd begun!

One frosty, bright morning, without any warning,
A dark line hove up from the mist;
It was Newfoundland's coast that we coveted most,
As did Pilgrims, 4 centuries past!

In a somber, cold meeting at Halifax's greeting,
Slow tallies were made, head by head,
But the seamen who started scarce eclipsed the departed,
And the day's count belonged to the dead.

Thus, the story is ending—a tale of befriending
And also of bravery and grief;
It ends where it started—among the brave hearted,
Whose moments of triumph were brief.

What had all gone before: a mad rush down to war
With its terror and bomb-bursting pall—
To go there and learn, and then, chastened, return,
The stern Murmansk Run topped them all.

Appendix II

SS ELDENA MERCHANT CREW[27]

List contributed by Jos Odijk of the Netherlands, a PQ-13 researcher, whose Uncle Niek Odijk died of exposure in a lifeboat after the bombing of the SS Raceland.

Nielsen, Ole M. Captain/ Master American 56
Bentley, Charles Chief Mate/ Chief Officer Am. 48
Lee, Henry W. 2nd Mate/ 2nd Officer American 62
Ford, Alexander 3rd Mate/ 3rd Officer American 35
Phelps, Giles Radio Operator American 19
Wood, John Boatswain/ Bosun American 30
Augensen, Valentin Carpenter Norwegian 47
Blanco, Peter Able-Bodied Seaman American 37
Donahue, William Able-Bodied Seaman American 21
Hunt, William Able-Bodied Seaman American 35
Jacobs, Reginald Able-Bodied Seaman American 24
Joy, Jesse Able-Bodied Seaman American 36
Palmer, Frank Able-Bodied Seaman American 36
Romano, Nunzia Ordinary Seaman American 29
Udiljak, Joseph Ordinary Seaman American 27
Lasslo, Steve Ordinary Seaman American 23
Bain, Gilbert 1st Eng. /Chief Eng. Officer Scottish 58
Barton, Clive 1st Assistant engineer American 38
Tompkins, Ottie W. 2nd Eng. /2nd Eng. Officer Am. 55
Nelson, Christian 3rd Eng. / 3rd Eng. Officer Am. 53
Donnelly, Frank 4th Engineer American 44
Mench, Algert Fireman American 23
Motylinski, Felix Fireman American 28
Sutton, Thomas Fireman American 26
Doxtator, Frank Oiler/Greaser American 53
Hoke, James Oiler/Greaser American 33
Robinson, Henry Oiler/Greaser American 32
Babkowski, Theodore Wiper American 23

Pasinosky, Joseph Wiper American 26
Lucas, Michael Steward American 55
Cans, Charles Chief Cook American 58
Hill, Christopher 2nd cook American 48
Bergman, Paysex Messman American 46
Igoe, Edward Messman American 28
Robertson, Alfred Messman British 38
Sheeks, Addison Messman American 36
White, Edward Messman American 26

Appendix III

In the Navy, a Mustang is an Officer who has promoted up from the ranks of Navy enlisted personnel through an in-service procurement program, with no interruption of his/her active duty status. It is also understood that the Mustang Officer was a career Sailor, and normally wears one or more Good Conduct Medals.

Thus, the Navy Mustang is either a Navy Limited Duty Officer (LDO), a Chief Warrant Officer (CWO), or commissioned through the Direct Fleet Accession, Seaman to Admiral (S2A) program, or the Naval Flight Officer program.[28]

BIBLIOGRAPHY

Brown, Roy W. *Jig How*, Baltimore, MD, Publish America, 2003

Fink, Fred S., Ensign USNR, *Voyage Report SS Eldena*, National Archives, Annapolis, MD, 1942

Gleichauf, Justin F. *Unsung Sailors*. Annapolis, MD, Naval Institute Press, 2002

Haynes, John L. *Haynes-McDonald Heritage Quest*. Anchorage, AK, McNaughton & Gunn, 1995

Lawson, Siri Holm, *Ships in Arctic Convoys*. www.warsailors.com/convoys/pq13.html

Lloyd, Charles A., USN Armed Guard WWII Veterans

Mills, Morris O. *Convoy PQ13 Unlucky for Some*, West Sussex,UK, Bernard Durnford, 2000

Morrison, Samuel Eliot. *The Battle of the Atlantic*, Champaign, IL., University of Illinois Press, 2001

Myers, Steve C., Captain USN, *Murmansk Run*. Bedford, PA. AG and MM Board

Odijk, Jos, of the Netherlands, a PQ-13 researcher

Smith, Gordon, http://www.naval-history.net/

Torgersen, Herman, Norwegian seamen. Excerpts from *Survivor Report SS Raceland*, 1942 www.warsailors.com/convoys/pq13.html

History of the US Naval Armed Guard Afloat-WWII OP-414 Cp II, *The North Russian Run* 1942

History of WWII, UK, The War at Sea, Cp IV, *Home waters and the Arctic*. 1942
Uboat.net, *Ships sunk by U-boats*, http://www.uboat.net/

Navy Mustang Association

MEMBERSHIP CERTIFICATE
Greetings Hear All Present,
This Certifies that
LCDR John L. Haynes USNR (Ret)
Has Satisfactorily Met The
Membership Requirements Of The Navy Mustang Association.
In recognition of superior leadership skills, the above named officer, has risen from the enlisted ranks and has therefore earned the title
"Mustang"
NMA-1992   November 13, 2009

* * *

NSSAR

John Haynes is a member to the National Society, Sons of the American Revolution and is a Past President of the Alaska State Society.

* * *

During the research for his book, *HAYNES-McDONALD—HERATIGE QUEST* written in 1995 he discovered that eight of his ancestors had fought in the American Revolution. They are:
Peter Neese, Frederick Mayberry, George Mayberry, Robert Skelton, Richard Woolley, John McMullan, Lewis Stowers, and Lewis Bobo.

NOTES

[1] Unsung Sailors by Justin F. Gleichauf, pp. 160, 161
[2] Unsung Sailors by Justin F. Gleichauf, pp. 95
[3] "Convoy PQ13 Unlucky for Some" by Morris O. Mills, pp. 90-91
[4] "Convoy PQ13 Unlucky for Some" by Morris O. Mills, pp. 91
[5] Excerpts from "Jig How" by Roy W. Brown, pp.60
[6] Excerpts from the survivor report of Norwegian seamen Herman Torgersen
[7] Voyage report by C.O. Ensign Fink May 9, 1942
[8] "Convoy PQ13 Unlucky for Some" by Morris O. Mills, pp. 95-96
[9] Uboat.net, Ships hit by U-boats
[10] Gordon Smith http://www.naval-history.net/
[11] "Convoy PQ-13 Unlucky for Some" by Morris O. Mills, pp.100
[12] Unsung Sailors by Justin F. Gleichauf, pp. 220-1
[13] Voyage report by C.O. Ensign Fink May 9, 1942
[14] "Convoy PQ13 Unlucky for Some" by Morris O. Mills, pp 103
[15] Voyage report by C.O. Ensign Fink May 9, 1942
[16] "Convoy PQ13 Unlucky for Some" by Morris O. Mills, pp 132
[17] History of the Naval Armed Guard Afloat-WWII OP-414, pp. 24, 25
[18] "Convoy PQ13 Unlucky for Some" by Morris O. Mills, pp. 118
[19] History of WWII, UK, The War at Sea, Cp IV, Home waters and the Arctic, pp. 128
[20] History of WWII, UK, The War at Sea, Cp IV, Home waters and the Arctic, pp. 129
[21] History of WWII, UK, The War at Sea, Cp IV, Home waters and the Arctic, pp. 129

[22] http://en.wikipedia.org/wiki/HMS_Edinburgh
[23] History of WWII, UK, The War at Sea, Cp IV, Home waters and the Arctic, pp. 129
[24] History of WWII, UK, The War at Sea, Cp IV, Home waters and the Arctic.
[25] http://www.armed-guard.com/about-mm.html
[26] Voyage report by C.O. Ensign Fink May 9, 1942
[27] *Jos Odijk of the Netherlands, a PQ-13 researcher*
[28] http://navymustangs.com/